SAVING THE FARM

"A practical guide to the legal maze of aging in America."

by

Greg McIntyre, J.D., M.B.A.

Elder Law Attorney

SAVING THE FARM
by Greg McIntyre

Copyright © 2016 by Greg McIntyre

ISBN-13: 978-1533642707

ISBN-10: 1533642702

Disclaimer:

Attorney Greg McIntyre is an elder law attorney and is licensed as an attorney in the State of North Carolina. Mr. McIntyre cannot give legal advice outside of the State of North Carolina. Some of the concepts discussed in this book may or may not be valid under the laws of other states. This book may serve as a guide and a framework to assist in you and/or your family's aging journey. It is recommended that you consult an estate planning and/or elder law attorney in your state to discuss specific legal issues. Feel free to contact Mr. McIntyre to inquire about legal issues and if needed, he or his office will route you to a reputable estate planning and elder law attorney in your state.

Contact Greg McIntyre, Elder Law Attorney at the following:

Phone: 704-259-7040

Website: *mcelderlaw.com*

Email: *greg@mcelderlaw.com*

Address: PO Box 165, Shelby, NC 28151

Furthermore, the information and concepts in this book in no way forms an attorney/client relationship when read by the reader. No legal advice is being conveyed or given under an attorney/client relationship in this book. The only way to form that attorney/client relationship would be to hire Mr. McIntyre or another attorney to perform legal work for you.

That being said, **ENJOY THE BOOK!!!** We think there is some great information within that will greatly benefit you and your family.

ACKNOWLEDGEMENTS

I have to first thank my mother, **Terry McIntyre**, who through late nights, critiqued and helped me edit this book. Mom has always had superior command of the English language. Thank you and I love you.

I must give many thanks to **Adam Butler**, who has been my friend since childhood and edited my book without complaint. Willingly. What a great friend and person.

To **Robert Ashford** (the Brit) who is great at helping me flow and contributed tons to this book.

To **Bob DeMers**... Thanks Bob for being my guru and helping me plan both my life, my business and this book.

Many thanks go to my office who without I could not function, serve clients, write books or feed my family. Many thanks to you all. You are a smart, hardworking, creative and dedicated group of men and women and I am blessed to know and work with you.

I must thank the wonderful crew at Elder Counsel who have always been there through my journey as an elder law attorney to answer questions and guide me along the way.

My Colleagues are owed many thanks and praises. They put up with me (sometimes)... answering my endless questions no matter how petty, deep or ridiculous.

Last but not least, I must thank my beautiful wife and our six awesome kids who never discourage me from writing, working late, chasing tangents or any other endeavor I decide to pursue. You are my rocks and my supports and I could do nothing without you.

FOREWORD

Elder Law attorneys care greatly for their senior clients and like to see things go smoothly for them, especially as difficult issues arise, such as finding and paying for long-term care. Clients who understand the need to plan early are more likely to find a smooth path into these transitions.

While typical estate planning includes planning for incapacity during one's lifetime as well as distribution of one's assets upon their passing, Elder Law attorneys have an added focus of planning with long-term care in mind. Often a traditional estate plan will have the same documents that an Elder Law attorney puts in place, like a Revocable Living Trust; a Pour-Over Will; a Durable Power of Attorney; a Health Care Power of Attorney; and a HIPAA Authorization. However, the provisions within the documents vary significantly depending on the focus of the attorney drafting them. Because one focus of the Elder Law attorney is to help clients plan for the possibility of needing long-term care while protecting the home and other assets, our planning documents often include an irrevocable trust designed specifically for this purpose. Other documents, like the Durable Power of Attorney, will include enhanced powers that allow the agent to engage in Medicaid and/or Veterans Administration ("VA") pension planning.

Adding enhanced provisions to existing planning documents enables those trusted persons to pursue additional planning strategies if and when the time comes for the senior to utilize long-term care. When the time comes for Medicaid planning or VA pension planning, it is imperative for the trustee and/or the agent to have the authority to take specific actions on behalf of the elderly person, like the authority to establish and fund an irrevocable trust, file a Medicaid application or prepare a VA pension application. The grant of authority must be clearly stated within the documents yet these powers are not normally found in general estate-planning documents.

Having clients in our office long before they are in need of long-term care allows Elder Law attorneys to successfully and efficiently assist clients when they need it. We are all thankful when we have such a client.

An Elder Law attorney's office is much more than a place where legal analysis is conducted or where legal documents are prepared. It is also a place where seniors are heard, encouraged to express all of the issues they are facing, and where connections are made.

We are thankful to have ongoing relationships with other professionals that are compassionate about the elderly. Our clients are much better off because of these other professionals. For example, many times a Placement Specialist is needed to help a client find the best facility to meet their long-term care needs. Sometimes a family needs a Care Manager for a variety of reasons including to act as an advocate or to oversee care provided to a loved one. Professional Fiduciaries can be an amazing resource for families as they can alleviate stress from family members allowing family to just "be there" for the senior. CPAs, Financial Advisors, other Estate Planning attorneys, Real Estate agents, Insurance agents and a plethora of other senior-centric professionals are invaluable to the Elder Law attorney devoted to their clients.

These relationships are not only personally fulfilling, but also allow us to comprehensively serve our clients.

There are many non-profit organizations that are dedicated to making life better for the elderly and who support Elder Law attorneys and for that we are thankful. These organizations keep us up to date on the issues facing the elderly, give us a heads up on changes in the laws across the country and continue to provide new ideas on how to best serve our clientele. The National Association of Elder Law Attorneys, the Alzheimer's Association and the National Council on Aging are a few of the organizations that Elder Law attorneys can connect with to better serve our clients. We are all in this together and working toward a common goal to serve seniors and their loved ones the best way possible.

Although we occasionally serve an elderly client who has no family members or close friends, we are thankful when trustworthy and committed family members are available to the client.

Many of the strategies we have available to us only work when a client has trusted people to assist in the strategy. Many thanks go to adult children who are committed to their parents. Spouses who are still devoted to your ill spouse after "how-many-ever" years of marriage are also greatly appreciated by Elder Law attorneys! Without you, our work would be much more difficult. Without you, the strategies we employ would fail to work the way they are meant to work. You are vital to the health and welfare of your elderly loved one.

It is often the family member who finds the Elder Law Attorney for the elderly client. As technology changes, the older client sometimes has a difficult time finding the necessary resources. We are very grateful to those family members who seek out an Elder Law attorney and bring us together.

Advocating for a senior can be stressful for a variety of reasons. While it is one of the most fulfilling jobs we can think of, it brings with it concerns for our clients that can creep up at all hours of the night. As with any professional whose heart is a big part of their service, our support systems are essential to our well-being.

Our support systems include our family members, professional colleagues, neighbors and our friends. Without our supporters, we would be unable to continue doing what we love.

Interactive Content:

You may find the corresponding audio and video interviews on mcelderlaw.com. The eBook version of this book features this content integrated within the book itself.

TABLE OF CONTENTS

CHAPTER 1

What on Earth Is Elder Law and Why Is It So Important?

What on Earth Is Elder Law?

At the heart of Elder Law is a philosophy of keeping a senior in control of their money and property while affording them healthcare and long-term care options during their golden years. Elder law is the practice of law providing tools for seniors to get their affairs in order so they can enjoy life, have peace of mind and leave a legacy for their children and grandchildren.

Elder law is not just for the elderly. You should begin planning to protect your hard-earned money and property and make sure you have a variety of healthcare options available as early as possible. Everyone should have powers of attorney for property and for healthcare decisions. These documents put you in control of this and help avoid the cost of drawn out court guardianship proceedings.

Why is Elder Law So Important?

There was once a young man who lived in Lattimore, North Carolina, who was recently married and though he had little formal education, was still a smart fellow. He was a hard worker who wanted nothing more than to take care of his family, so he found a job as a tenant farmer. A tenant farmer is someone who works land in exchange for room, board, and payment, such as money or a portion of the crops collected.

As a newly-wed the young man worked the entire year to bring in the crops. When they were harvested and sold, the landowner took the crops, and the profit, sharing none of it. The young farmer needed his share of the monies collected to support and feed his wife and growing family, yet he received nothing.

He was not discouraged however, and kept working as a tenant farmer for years. He also worked for a furniture maker and discovered he had quite a talent for making custom furniture with intricate detail and carvings. He continued to use this talent throughout his life until he was able buy his own land and home in Mooresboro, North Carolina, complete with a workshop for his woodworking equipment. This is where they lived and raised six children. At this time, he began working for Daniels Construction Company at Fiber Industries in Earl, North Carolina, staying there for around twenty years.

After he retired and the children had left and married, he and his wife sold the two story house in Mooresboro and bought land and a one level home in Lattimore. Too soon after this, his wife died in her early 60's. In the wake of her death, he lost interest in life itself, auctioned the house they shared, most of the handcrafted furniture, their collection of antiques, reserving only one piece of hand crafted furniture for each child. For the next ten years he lived in his children's homes.

Then after years of neglecting his health, he became very ill and fell into a coma for three months. He went into respiratory arrest on three occasions but was shocked back to life. This was followed by a short stay in a nursing home. The hospital and nursing home care costs were astronomical.

Unfortunately, he was neither a lawyer nor a financial planner, and lived in a time where planning for a catastrophic health care event, nursing home care, assisted living care, or in-home care was not often contemplated. He had little money set aside to take care of his long-term, assisted living or skilled nursing care needs. His children could keep only enough of the man's savings for a burial fund of $10,000. Everything else had to go toward those bills. This was required by Medicaid at the time for paying for his assisted living care. He wasn't even allowed to own a home. Even if he hadn't auctioned the farm house after the death of his wife, he would still have been required to pay for his assisted living care.

That man was Worth McIntyre, my grandfather, whom I affectionately referred to as Pa Pa Mac. He lived in assisted living care for the last ten years of his life until he passed away. Pa Pa Mac did not have the foresight to put aside money for his long-term health care needs.

To my knowledge, there were no readily available and affordable financial industry products to help pay for long-term care needs either. Pa Pa Mac was in a position where his hard work – the money and property he had worked so hard for his entire life – was taken from him toward the end. This is a story I hear regularly when giving seminars and through my law practice. This is not the exception but more the norm these days.

Because of these stories, I have a passion for helping individuals and families keep their hard earned money and property, and retain control of it during their lifetime, and pass it to their loved ones so they may leave a legacy.

SAVING THE FARM

When I was growing up, the Cold War with Russia was still ongoing. Russia was a place where all property was owned by, or went back to the government. One thing that makes us American is the ability to hold onto money and property and to pass it on generation after generation.Today however, the money and property of individuals requiring long-term care are liquidated en masse due to our governmental policies.These individuals did not take the proper steps to protect what they worked so hard to earn.

What is happening with the assets of our senior population equates to the wholesale redistribution of property in a country founded in part on the right of individuals to own and pass property. Individuals should be able to keep their hard-earned money and property, control it while alive, and pass it on to their loved ones so the next generation might have it easier than they did.

According to a 2005 report on long-term care conducted by the U.S. Department of Health and Human Services, approximately 70% of people over 65 will need some type of long term care during their lifetime[1]. That's twelve (12) million Americans expected to need long-term care in the year 2020[2]. The average length of nursing home stays according to the American Association of Long-Term Care Insurance's 2008 Sourcebook are broken down as follows:

[1]http://longtermcare.gov/the-basics/who-needs-care/
[2]http://news.morningstar.com/articlenet/article.aspx?id=564139

Average Length of Stays (Nursing Homes)	
5 years or more	12.0%
3 to 5 years	12.0%
1 to 3 years	30.3%
6 to 12 months	14.2%
3 to 6 months	10.0%
less than 3 months	20.0%
Average Length of Stay in Years	
Female	2.6 years
Male	2.3 years
Married	1.6 years
Single / Never Married	3.8 years
Widowed	2.3 years
Divorced / Separated	2.7 years

[3]The U.S. Department of Health and Human Services website, LongTermCare.gov, provides average costs for long-term care in the United States (in 2010):

▶ $205 per day or $6,235 per month for a semi-private room in a nursing home

▶ $229 per day or $6,965 per month for a private room in a nursing home

▶ $3,293 per month for care in an assisted living facility (for a one-bedroom unit)

▶ $21 per hour for a home health aide

▶ $19 per hour for homemaker services

▶ $67 per day for services in an adult day health care center

The cost of long-term care depends on the type and duration of care you need, the provider you use, and where you live. Costs can be affected by certain factors, such as:

▶ Time of day. Home health and home care services, provided in two-to-four-hour blocks of time referred to as "visits," are generally more expensive in the evening, on weekends, and on holidays

▶ Extra charges for services provided beyond the basic room, food and housekeeping charges at facilities, although some may have "all inclusive" fees.

▶ Variable rates in some community programs, such as adult day service, are provided at a per-day rate, but can be more based on extra events and activities[4].

It is easy to see how the costs of an average nursing home stay of 2.6 years for a female, at an average yearly price tag of $83,580 will deplete even a large amount of retirement savings fast.

[3]http://www.aaltci.org/long-term-care-insurance/learning-center/probability-long-term-care.php
[4] http://longtermcare.gov/costs-how-to-pay/costs-of-care/

I am extremely grateful for the advances in modern science and medical technology. Everyone wants a long and healthy life. But at what cost. There has to be a better way.

There are cost-effective strategies for helping individuals save their money and property, and I am extremely passionate about this because of what I witnessed with my grandfather. My mission is to help individuals save the farm– to help them save their dignity.

Imagine working for 30, 40, or 50 years to pay off a mortgage and a home equity loan, to be free of debt, only to have a catastrophic health event take that home away in a very short time. That is the reality of our modern world, coupled with the large and aging baby boomer population.

In this book, we will explore ways to protect your finances–from foundational concepts to more advanced planning strategies. We will explore the many ways to save the farm.

Could my grandfather and his family have avoided losing his hard earned money and property? How many out there are in the same position? What might have happened if he and his family had known there were legal options? "Knowledge is Power[5] ." How many people could avoid those pitfalls using that knowledge? If only they knew their healthcare options and how to protect their assets. Each chapter will empower you with this knowledge.

The goal of this book is to help keep the individual in charge of his or her money and property until it comes time to pass it on to the next generation. My ultimate aim is to help those individuals keep their dignity and pass on a legacy.

[5] Sir Francis Bacon, Meditationes Sacrae and Human Philosophy (1597).

SAVING THE FARM

CHAPTER 2

Foundations of Elder Law Planning

I f the anecdote about my grandfather teaches you anything, it's that planning is crucial. The steps you take right now to ensure that you and your family hold onto the hard-earned money and assets will only benefit you and your loved ones in the future. I therefore, dedicate this chapter to methods of planning and preparation. This includes the documents and people vital in your quest to save the farm and all your legacies that come with it. These components include what I consider the foundations or pillars of elder law planning: The first pillar is the General Durable Power of Attorney, the second pillar is the Healthcare Power of Attorney, and wills such as a Living Will is the third pillar.

General Durable Power of Attorney

The first of the documents you need in your arsenal is known as a General Durable Power of Attorney (referred to as DPA). I'm sure you have heard of a Power of Attorney, and might have acted as one in your life. A Power of Attorney is the document that enables someone of your choosing to act on your behalf. From a legal standpoint, this document normally becomes void when you become disabled, incapacitated, incompetent or pass away.

There is, however, another Power of Attorney that many people consider in their old age. Known as a General Durable Power of Attorney, this kind differs slightly from the one described above. A General Durable Power of Attorney- which I will refer to as a DPA – states that the terms under which the designated individual can act are not limited to a person's disability, incapacity or incompetence but is terminated only when the principal passes away. Here is what I mean: say an older man (known as the 'Principle') names an individual close to him in his DPA. Not long after, the 'Principal' becomes incapacitated due to a health incident, and can no longer make decisions for himself due to his situation. The designated individual (known as the 'Attorney in Fact') in the DPA can still make decisions on the 'Principle's' behalf, even though the 'Principal' has become incapacitated. The actions that are allowed and the powers granted still hold, and these extend until the 'Principal' passes away; simply put, the terms follow the 'Principal' until his last day.

I encourage you to ask yourself the following questions:

- ▶ If you were to suffer a healthcare incident that rendered you incapacitated, what financial losses do you expect you would experience?
- ▶ What important affairs in your life would need overseeing?
- ▶ Who would you trust to oversee them?

These are the questions that should guide your decision in signing a DPA. Without one, your family and loved ones will go through a long and arduous process - one that may involve going to court - in hopes of regaining control of your important affairs.

It is also important that you understand the two types of DPAs, which are as follows:

Immediate DPA:

This one is self-explanatory, a General Durable Power of Attorney goes into effect the second the document is signed. Thus, the DPA is immediately effective.

Springing DPA:

This type of General Durable Power of Attorney takes effect once an incident occurs in which the designated individual has to take action. For example, if a 'Principal' is in a car accident and the designee must then take responsibility for the 'Principal's' property and other possessions, the DPA has "sprung" into effect. When we talk about health care incidents and planning, this is one of the more widely chosen types of DPA.

The crucial thing to remember about DPAs is that the 'Principal' must be absolutely coherent and functioning at full mental capacity in order to sign the DPA. Given that, the DPA provides for a trusted individual to take over and handle important life affairs if the 'Principal' can no longer function in that coherent mental state for whatever reason. In addition, the actions and responsibilities that the designated individual can take must be outlined by the 'Principal'; under the DPA, a designated person can only act within the constraints established by the document, something which will differ for each DPA as these are very specific terms.

Healthcare Power of Attorney

While the responsibilities of General DPAs refer to different actions that the 'Attorney in Fact' can take, there is a more specific type of Power of Attorney I will explore in this section: The Healthcare Power of Attorney. The Healthcare Power of Attorney is how it sounds: It's a Power of Attorney that exercises his or her power in matters relating to healthcare. Due to the nature of these decisions, I highly recommend that your Healthcare Power of Attorney be as specific as possible in its language. This will put healthcare professionals more at ease when they interact with your 'Attorney in Fact'; they will feel much more comfortable having your 'Attorney in Fact' follow the guidelines of your Power of Attorney. As always, be sure that your 'Attorney in Fact' is a trusted individual. If you suddenly become mentally unable to make decisions about your own health, who would you want to make those decisions for you?

Vacationing and Healthcare Directives

At the end of July 2015, my family and I spent a week at Litchfield Beach and Golf Resort in Litchfield, South Carolina, where I spent a few days playing a little golf and spending time on the beach with my family. The year before, I took my wife and children to a resort called Rumbling Bald, in the mountains of North Carolina 45 minutes from where I practice. Despite the short drive, Rumbling Bald felt a world away from what I am used to seeing each day.

While on these vacations I wrote an article about the importance of having a healthcare power of attorney and living will in place when traveling away from home. It is never a good idea to go anywhere unprepared, not even your vacation. Healthcare incidents do not wait patiently for you to return from your week on the beach with your family; you know surprises happen at any point, regardless of where you are or who is with you. It is for this reason we need these foundational documents in place.

Now, I'll admit I am not exempt from failing to plan, and I'm sure many of you are the same. Sometimes I am working 100% to make sure others are protected and neglect getting my own affairs in order. I'm striving very hard to provide for my family and ensure my kids can go to college, but it's also very important that I have my own situation handled. That means setting up my various powers of attorney and my living will, especially when traveling. Should something happen, I'd want to show those to a doctor in this area.

Should I have an accident or be in a bad situation, I'd want no question about what should be done and who makes those decisions. At McIntyre Elder Law, we are very proud of our eDocs access system that places your most important legal documents right at your fingertips, no matter where you are. Our eDocs access card allows you to view all of your critical information from anywhere. It features bank level security, so just like your online banking, you can have your important legal papers stored securely online. We happily provide that service for our clients.

If you are anything like me, you do not have all your legal documents on you in paper form at all times. With the eDocs service that we offer, these documents can be pulled up and the hospital's doctor and staff can see all of your healthcare directives. Using myself as an example, should I ever be in a situation where I'm in a persistent vegetative state, brain dead, or something of that nature, this will provide them with everything they need to know: who my power of attorney is, who may make important healthcare decisions for me, do I want to be maintained by machines, receive artificial hydration or nutrition, and things of that nature.

Should I be traveling alone, my next of kin can grant access by e-mail and a link is provided. It does not send the documents as an attachment and expose it to the Internet, instead it gives a secure log-in where they can be accessed. You can provide a log-in to a son, daughter, trusted adviser, or wife so they can have access to those legal documents. If you want your children to view those healthcare documents and powers of attorney but not the will or trust documents also on your eDocs log-in, you can use the system to grant and restrict access to those different areas.

Just as you check the oil in your car before you go on vacation, you need to check your legal documents to make sure you have your Healthcare Powers of Attorney, your General Durable Power of Attorney, your Living Will, and your Will in place and set before going on vacation. Summer is a great time to go on vacation, and hang out with family, but what happens if you and your wife travel maybe to Tennessee, maybe to the mountains or the beach – and the unexpected happens? As we discussed in this chapter, we want to make sure you have those healthcare documents and your directives with you through our eDocs program. These documents are at your fingertips on any device, from your laptop to smartphone, so the hospital, wherever you are, will know who makes healthcare decisions for you. You could have those documents ready at the healthcare facility, for the doctors and nurses.

Living Wills

The third foundational pillar is the Living Will, also called a Declaration for a Desire for a Natural Death. People feel strongly about these documents due to experience and deeply held religious beliefs. Heaven forbid you should find yourself in the unfortunate situation where you are terminal, incurable, brain death has occurred for example, and you're only being maintained by artificial machinery, hydration, and nutrition. What do you want to happen in that situation? Do you want to continue on indefinitely? Do you want a chance to recover? Would you want to choose while you are competent, how the doctor and nurses should handle that situation? Do you want your Healthcare Power of Attorney to make that decision? Do you want your kids to make that decision? Or do you take that guilt-ridden decision and make it yourself and say, "This is my statement of intent and this is what I want to happen"? A Living Will, or a Declaration for a Desire for a Natural Death, puts you in control of one of life's most important decisions.

Wills

It's all too common for clients to think that just because we are an Elder Law firm, we do wills. My answer to those people is, yes we do wills, but ask yourself, is a will really what you need? In this section, I was going to suggest that wills might be obsolete. That statement will probably shock you, considering everyone always says, 'you need to have a will'. If you do not, who will receive your valuable possessions? A question like that comes up countless times between family members. Yet are you absolutely clear about the perils and pitfalls of passing things by Will?

Though my answer might be arresting, here's the truth: you do not necessarily need a will. In fact, if I do my job right, the last thing you'll do is pass down your property through a will. Why is that? Well, a Will is still a functional document to pass property for many people. It is an important document to have, but is what I commonly refer to as a safety net. A will can catch anything we don't pass directly. But it also carries pitfalls that catch you if you're not careful.

Types of Wills

First, I want to differentiate between standard Wills and Living Wills before I move into the pitfalls that can occur with drafting these documents. A standard Will by definition is a contract, either written or spoken, that provides for a few things to happen when you die. Specifically, a standard Will should address the following:

Distribution of property and assets.

A will as most people know will identify the recipients of any property or assets you own. These are the beneficiaries you must specify in your Will, for they will receive everything you leave to them as per your outlined terms. You are also responsible for delineating which beneficiary receives what asset.

Dependent children.

If you have children under the age of 18, you will want to name a legal guardian for that child / children upon your death.

The Executor.

The person you designate as an executor will be responsible for distributing your assets and property, and will take control of your finances after you pass away. The executor retains control of paying your taxes and any debts you might owe.

The standard Will differs from a Living Will, which is also known as an Advance Directive. As part of a living will, you may designate how you are cared for in an end of life medical situation. This commonly includes whether to resuscitate and what types of medications you will allow the doctors to give you if you become unable to verbalize that information to them. If you do not have a Living Will and you fall into a comatose or a vegetative state, the hospitals will turn to a family member to decide whether to resuscitate or not. The benefit of having a Living Will is that it guarantees you will remain on artificial nutrition or life support if you so wish.

There are, however, some pitfalls to a Living Will. The first is the terminology used in the actual document. Say for example you use the word "incapacitated" in your Living Will to describe the terms under which your document goes into effect. If you are not specific in your language, there might be inconsistencies between doctors on what "incapacitated" means. Does it mean you are comatose? That you cannot feed yourself? Are you completely clear so that if the time comes, there's no question what actions the hospital should take?

The other disadvantage - which I touched on when speaking about vacationing and your documents - is that many of us keep our Living Wills somewhere other than the hospital where we are staying. Of course, you have to expect this. If a freak accident happens, you are not expected to be carrying around your Living Will. Yet the problem that arises when doctors and healthcare providers do not have access to your Living Will is they might not honor it if they don't know it exists. For this reason, it is crucial you have some way of informing your doctors and healthcare providers that the Living Will exists. Perhaps you would want to inform your family, and let them know how to access it and pass it on to the doctors or the hospital. As I have stated, planning and preparation is key. This also includes the people you choose to make a part of your process.

Executors: Every Ship Needs a Captain

An executor is much like the captain of a ship and the probate process is comparable to navigating through sometimes treacherous open ocean. You want to stay out of trouble in these legal waters, and by having the right executor helping you with every estate plan, you will avoid certain dangers. An executor gets you to where you are going with the least amount of difficulty.

An executor is not to be confused with an administrator, the difference being you appoint an executor through your will and an administrator is chosen by the clerk of court in the event you haven't prepared one at the time of your passing. This is known as Dying Intestate.

Why is establishing an executor so important? An executor is in charge of making sure your property gets to the person you intend it for. You'll also need to designate a secondary executor who will take the initial executor's place in the event he or she becomes disabled, incapacitated, not in good health, or declines the job when it's time to carry out your wishes. Think of the secondary executor as someone waiting on deck in case the primary executor cannot perform his or her job.

A key attribute to look for in a potential executor is trustworthiness. You want someone you can count on to captain your ship and avoid the icebergs out there. You've spent time planning your legacy and making the right choices, building your ship from the ground up. All that hard work could disappear in an instant if you do not set sail with the right captain. It is, therefore, important to choose wisely or your plan could sink.

When thinking of this, there will likely be a short list of people that come to mind. It (the executor) may be a trusted friend, or a family member who is financially responsible and could be trusted with your estate.

There are things you want to think about when allowing this person to serve as your executor. You might let them serve without bond so they don't have to be bonded by an insurance company.

Insurance companies will provide an insurance bond to your executor but at a price to the executor. This bond could be paid back to the executor later in the probate process. However, if you specify that your executor may serve without bond then the executor has no need to spend money with an insurance company in connection with your estate. Bonding is generally required during the probate process to protect the assets of the estate from being used by the executor for any other purpose than that which you specify in your will. Should your executor choose to pay off their own credit cards with your money which is not given them under your Will, the insurance company would pay back the estate in this case. So, you should carefully consider whether the executor you appoint requires bonding or not.

You could give them power to sell land at a public or private auction. This allows them to more easily liquidate or move property through your estate. This also helps to avoid drawn out legal battles caused by disagreements between family members or 'Petitions to Partition' (lawsuits to split property that could occur). These are a few things you should think about and discuss with your attorney while drafting a Will and picking an executor.

Now that you understand the importance of an executor, where should you start? Begin by creating a plan of action. First, seek legal counsel. Next, speak with them about having a will drafted. There's an old saying that goes, "there's no such thing as a simple Will." The counsel you select should be able to tell you about the potential dangers you'll face and whether a simple Will meets your needs.

Come in prepared to name an executor, someone you trust. Your child or other family member, or a close friend who you think will be a great captain of your ship. You can also consider appointing co-executors, though having a single leader executing the final orders is often an easier way to avoid squabbling and in-fighting.

How to Avoid Liens on Your Estate

Now we're clear on the different types of wills and the people to involve, I want to make you aware of the various pitfalls that can emerge in the realm of Wills, specifically in talking about your estate.

Let's talk about the perils of the probate estate first. Liens can attach to property you pass by Will. In North Carolina, where I practice law, there is a 90-day publication requirement or waiting period—depending on the size of the estate—for liens or bills to be filed on the open estate.

If bills or liens come in on the estate, then the probate assets will be used if it is cash. If it is a house or something else as value, then it will be sold to settle those liens. As if that isn't traumatic enough an idea, remember that the selling or use of your probate assets occurs before the property is passed down to your heirs. Therefore, the house you thought would pass to your family through a Will may not actually go to them at all. If you have a medical lien hanging over that process, then there is a 90-day period in which that lien needs to be paid. The courts will require that those liens be paid before the heirs get their money.

If all you have in terms of assets is a house, then that will be sold to pay the price of the lien. Fortunately, there are ways to pass the house and other property – just like a beneficiary on a life insurance policy – outside of the estate, directly to your heir or whoever you want to receive that property. This type of direct, outside-of-estate administration strategy, could be done with your home. It may be accomplished using certain types of deeds. This transfer of real property could also be accomplished using trusts. Rest assured there are other ways to pass property in addition to a Will.

How to Keep Your Estate Private

That is one pitfall of using a Will. Wills are also public documents. So if you've got an estate and you don't want people seeing what's in it, or to know how you pass things along, avoid recording it or filing it at the courthouse because it is a public record. Anybody can look and see just how much of your property was passed.

Other ways to pass property, aside from going to the courthouse and filing a Will, would be to use a trust. Trusts are private documents. You could have an attorney, for instance, administer that trust with the family present – right in the office, right around the conference table. Wills are public documents and trusts are private documents.

Why Wills Are Still Necessary

With that being said, Wills are still part of the foundations you need in place. It's still a reliable document to make sure that whatever we plan to pass directly, transferable upon death, still passes and gets where you want it to go. But if you're doing proper planning, you're going to look at how to pass assets directly to your loved ones so that liens cannot attach, and nothing gets in the way.

You may say, "Well, I'm not going to owe anything at the end". Well it's my job to look at contingencies and plan to protect your assets. And that's what I do. So, if you're with me, I will tell you about potential harm that may come if you don't pass things directly or protect your assets properly.

Each day when I leave for work, I do so knowing that I have no idea whether I'll be in a car accident either on the way to the office or coming home. In North Carolina, for instance, there's a very low insurance threshold. The minimum policy limit for car insurance is 30/60. That means if one person is hurt in a wreck, the most they'll pay out is $30,000 if you carry minimum limits for liability. With multiple people – say a mom with 5 kids in the car – $60,000 is the most that policy would pay.

Car wrecks happen every day. They're a common occurrence. Heaven forbid, but if you get in an accident as you get older, $30,000 will not be enough to cover a serious injury. If your insurance doesn't cover it, that could roll over and become a lien on your probate estate. After you pass, that lien still needs to be paid and things may have to be sold to pay it. For that reason, we set up these kinds of protective measures, because there is always the potential for things like that to happen if we don't.

You don't know the shark's in the water until it bites you.

The Importance of Pre-Planning:
A Lesson from my Grandmother

In early April 2015, something happened in my life that forced me to think long and hard about how we can avoid crisis situations in our lives. That event was the passing of my grandmother, who lived into her mid-80s. I am comforted to say she passed away peacefully and with her sister holding her hand. She had not been sick very long, and luckily did not suffer.

I was always very close to my grandmother, and can remember spending almost the entirety of every summer over there at the house she owned with my grandfather, who passed away some time before she did. She was a sharp lady who worked her whole life, saved her money, and always left room for a smile on her face or a kind word for other people. The house I visited in the summer was one they owned and had managed to pay off. That reflects just how productive their life was.

Not only did my grandmother plan ahead with saving, she also planned to protect what she saved. I discovered she had deed work done in 2006 to protect her home, to ensure that no matter what happened to her, her home would never be sold to satisfy some medical debt or to pay for a nursing home, in-home, or assisted living care. My mother made sure that she, along with her brother and sister, had a Medical and General Durable Power of Attorney in place. They enacted these steps to guarantee they could handle or manage her affairs in between some of the healthcare incidents and events that befell my grandmother in her life. This included open heart surgery in 2004 and some other situations she was simply unable to manage in her life. They also enacted the DPA so they could continue to oversee the important matters toward the end of her life.

Having those Powers of Attorney in place meant the kids could step in and keep everything under control for her. They designated responsibility to trusted individuals who could handle her affairs and make sure the band played on, while she recovered. This level of planning made sure nobody dropped the ball paying bills and the doctors would not be wondering who to look to for healthcare matters. In addition, most of her liquid assets were set up in either joint accounts, with rights of survivorship, or transferable upon death assets that had beneficiaries. So at the end of her life, probating the estate wasn't much of an issue at all.

If I've learned anything from this event, it's that avoiding a crisis situation is crucial. In the event life throws you a curveball and a healthcare incident leaves you asking, "What now?" or fearing you will lose your liquid assets, it's important to organize things ahead of time. Even after her passing, my grandmother is still teaching me life lessons that I am pleased to share with you, so you may take the necessary precautions and steps to provide for your family the way my grandmother has provided for hers.

Pre-Need Funeral Planning

Though the thought is a morbid one, part of the essential planning process will be your pre-funeral plans that must be implemented after your passing. This process is known as Pre-Need Funeral Planning, and is a great benefits planning tool for long-term care Medicaid planning. Those who participate in this pre-planning opportunity can place $10,000 to $15,000 in a trust or insurance account with a reputable funeral home where that money is exempt from the Medicaid spend down. The unused portion is then distributed directly to the heirs/children of the deceased.

To gain more insight into this process, I interviewed Cecil Burton, a long-time friend of mine and owner of Cecil M. Burton

Funeral Home and Crematory. Cecil has been in the funeral home business for years. One can learn lots from him about the importance of pre-need funeral planning and why it's a vital part of planning as you age.

Interview with Cecil M. Burton, Funeral Home Owner and Director

Why is it important to choose the right funeral home to do your funeral planning and to do pre-needs funeral planning?

Well, it's essential that you pick the right funeral home because we're just like any profession, we have our good people and our bad people. Ninety percent of them are good and do a good job, but you need to inspect the facilities and make sure that the people have their licenses and are certified to do pre-planning because in the state of North Carolina you have to have a license to do pre-planned funerals.

In order to be a licensed funeral rep, you have to have two licenses to be able to do a pre-planned funeral. We have a lot of people who are pre-planning their funeral now just for Medicaid reasons, the spend down. We put the money into an insurance trust where it gets interest on your money but it's tax-free interest. We also do business with people who just want to pick out their stuff and lock in the price. We do that, too. You can pick your stuff, lock in the price, and it doesn't matter how long it takes, it's taken care of.

If somebody comes to you and says, "McIntyre at McIntyre Elder Law told me to come over here and I need to do a pre-needs funeral plan," go through the steps; what would you do for that person?

Well, we'd find out what their needs are. Sometimes they have brothers or sisters who want to be in the process of picking out a casket or the vault for the cremation, and they can't be here physically, so we'd help them. Then sometimes people want to just put money aside. We put that into a trust, and we trust 100% of the money and that way the money will get tax-free interest until the person passes away. For Medicaid, it has to be an irrevocable trust. This means they divorce themselves totally from that money; they can't get that money out until that person dies. The money will sit in interest and then if something does happen, they have the principle plus interest to pick out the casket, the vault for cremation services when the brothers and sisters can be in on it.

Now, we have some people where the brothers and sisters are local and they want to go ahead, come in, and pick out the casket and vault for the cremation services to go ahead and pay for it, lock in the price. We do it that way also. That's called inflation proof, which means you're locking in the price. If you just put money in, it's called a standard contract, which is the second type. Both of them for Medicaid have to be irrevocable. If you're not doing Medicaid, you can always make it revocable meaning you can get the money out anytime you want, interest plus principle.

As we discussed in the previous interview, pre-planning a funeral is not only a smart way to get your affairs in order, it's also a way to use your money for you. What do I mean by that? You are using your hard-earned money to pay for your burial expenses and not leave that burden for your children. Pre-needs burial planning is an acceptable way to spend your money even if you have a long-term care event in your future and need assistance from Medicaid to pay for that care.

In the next chapter we will explore the many different types of long-term care, and the real challenge many seniors face paying for it.

CHAPTER 3

What Is Long Term Care?

Throughout the health care and legal world, long term care is defined as the type of care and services provided to individuals who require special and individualized assistance following some type of healthcare incident. Normally, people seek this type of long term assistance if they become disabled through an injury, incur a chronic illness, or if they fall victim to a debilitating neurological disease, such as Alzheimer's. This assistance can include helping the individual perform basic functions and fulfill everyday tasks, such as bathing, eating, and moving around. Long term care is typically fulfilled by caregivers, and can be performed right in the individual's home if necessary. It is important to note that while some services may be free, others come at a cost to the patient.

One of the more gripping statistics regarding long term care was published in 2010, stating that 69% of the people who turned 65 back in 2005 are going to need some form of long term medical care. What does this figure mean to you? It means that, statistically speaking, you are most likely going to need some type of prolonged treatment, that is going to be a huge financial drain on your resources.

Even estates of a half-million to two million dollars could be drawn down to zero with the enormous costs of prolonged healthcare. This is especially so if that care involves some type of specialized treatment, in addition to a long-term care or nursing home facility. How can you prepare for or plan around this? You find somebody who can help you, someone that can plan around it.

We will delve into the different kinds of long term care that are available to you, with specific details on what they entail. For you, it is crucial you know what physical ailments require long term care. Temporary long term care, which could last only for a few weeks or months depending on the severity of the situation, includes rehabilitation after a surgery, an accident, or an illness. Then there is ongoing long term care - which lasts more than a few months and can be sustained for years - includes any illness that becomes chronic, any disability that looks to be permanent, or a health incident that renders the patient in need of constant or semi-constant supervision. As mentioned before, Alzheimer's falls under the category of an illness that might eventually require ongoing long term care. We will explore this gripping disease in detail later to clarify what happens, and how you can protect yourself and your loved ones should the illness become prevalent in your family.

Independent Living Facilities

An independent living facility is perfect for a senior citizen 55 years or over who is generally capable of taking care of day to day responsibilities. This option is the best for seniors who are mobile and do not require much oversight during the day or night. Seniors who are generally healthy, yet simply do not want to live alone in their own house or apartment - or seniors whose family members think they should be living in a community - can begin to live in these independent facilities. That way, the senior feels like he or she is still maintaining some independence, but is not completely alone. As many of the seniors who live in these facilities are not there for medical reasons, there is typically no regular medical care provided. That is an extra cost.

Independent living facilities offer a range of services and amenities to the people living there. Recreational centers might include workout areas, swimming pools, group fitness, and a whole host of other attractions. There are plenty of activities available to those who decide to live there.

Cost is going to be a factor in considering a move to an independent living facility. The national average monthly cost is going to be anywhere from $1,500 to $3,000, and Medicare will not cover these costs. Fortunately for some of the people who qualify, there are options for seniors who fall in the low-income economic bracket. The Department of Housing and Urban Development (HUD), provides housing complexes for seniors who qualify.

Assisted Living Facilities

Unlike independent living facilities, assisted living facilities are for people unable to live independently and take care of themselves without assistance. Most of the people who live in assisted living facilities have disabilities, and require aid with ADLs, or Activities of

Daily Living. This aid comes in the form of health care providers and trained facility staff to help with day-to-day needs. Assisted living facilities are often populated with individuals who, although they lack full independence, do not require round-the-clock supervision, and are perhaps too young to qualify to live in a retirement home or community.

The majority of individuals living in assisted living facilities are 85 years or older, with a small percentage of people under the age of 65. These facilities strive to provide a community feel, and offer similar services as one finds in an independent living facility. The responsibilities and tasks provided, include laundry, dressing, bathing, distribution and help with medication, cooking, and other basic tasks that the individual cannot complete on their own.

When it comes to cost, the average price for an assisted living facility is around $3,500 per month. It is important to note that this is the price for the lowest-tier room, meaning it's only a one-bedroom apartment as opposed to a two-bedroom or something larger. As with independent living facilities, the costs are not covered by Medicare.

Spotlight on: Brookdale Senior Living

Brookdale Senior Living is a premier nationwide provider of senior living services and has nearly 80,000 associates. Regional Vice President of Operations for Brookdale's Southeast Division, Kellee Agee, talks about assisted living, senior services, the future of the industry, and more.

How did you come to hold the position of Regional Vice President of Operations?

Such a wonderful story. As with anyone in healthcare, there is an interesting hook at some point in their lives. About 20 years ago now, a best friend of mine who was in assisted living as an executive director running a community, she and I would many times talk about our jobs. I was a business woman but I wasn't in healthcare but I had a tremendous amount of stress as she did, I dealt with laws, regulations, budgets, and employees. But she had such stories about having an impact with people's lives, and it spoke to me on such a level that when I became pregnant, I had a very early somewhat mid-life crisis where I felt I wanted to do something more meaningful. So I spoke to my family about wanting to get into senior living. But I was told I couldn't just come in and run without having experience in the healthcare aspect. I was willing to take a step back and become a part, so I was hired as the business manager of a community after I convinced them I was serious.

At that time, after about 4 months in the business office capacity, I was promoted to my own building, which is unheard of and I don't know anyone else who was that fast paced. But in North Carolina at the time, there wasn't any kind of formalized training or certification that you had to go through. From day one when I walked into the industry, I had to take home manuals to learn what people were saying around me. But looking back, I can't imagine doing anything else; I feel so privileged to care for people. It kind of chose me, I feel.

How many assisted living facilities do you have nationwide?

At Brookdale we've got a little over 1,100 properties. The region that I oversee has 35 properties across North Carolina and Virginia, and so that's my area of expertise at this given point. We have such tremendous heart at the head of this company, and you almost have to experience it. Our former CEO was such a tremendous man that set a benchmark of excellence and of being a person first, and allowing that to translate into what we do. Andy Smith, when he took the reins and getting the chance to see Andy respond, interact, and communicate with our company – as large as we are – he has continued that same standard. It's a privilege. We truly have people that understand the results come from doing the other things right and doing them well, and that you're going to have periods of time where there's going to be a lull.

If a family out there who is in need of an assisted living facility is looking for the right place for the father, mother, husband, etc., what should they look for in an assisted living community?

That's a great question, and I think it's something – to be honest with you – I wish more families would better equip themselves by visiting different communities. There's such an emotional state of mind when someone is in need of help or support with a loved one. They thus tend to put too much weight on how they connect with an individual person – be that a salesperson or a person in administration – and it needs to go beyond that. The people aspect is critical, so one of the things I tell my own family members and neighbors, people who don't have Brookdale as an option, is when they go into any healthcare setting, talk to and pay attention to all of the people within the walls of the community. Talk to as many as you can to get a sense of their satisfaction, their happiness.

What kind of feel do you get from people who are there day in and day out?

Definitely interact with the residents, if possible. Sometimes it's not as beneficial, but they will tell you if they are happy, engaged, if they're treated with respect from the staff. If that's not part of the initial walk-through, then take that initiative and try to talk to other people. Even with something like Brookdale, it's all about having great people who are called to do what they're doing, who are well trained, and who have the resources. You don't have to be overly-educated or understand all the jargon or ins and outs of regulations and requirements; it really comes down to a family going into a community and getting a sense of the people working within the community, and the confidence they can have. That makes the difference, and that's something that Brookdale understands; it's threaded in everything that we do, that people are the key. It's not the corporate office, it's not me, it's not having state-of-the-art programs; it's about investing in the caregiver, the cook, in the housekeeper. That's where you're going to get the most impact, in the people working within the community who are actually providing the care.

With the caregivers, you need to look into, are they certified by a state program? Are they actually required to be certified nursing assistants? Do they have nurses Monday through Friday? Do they have them around the clock? I think they need to be empowered to ask every hard-hitting question that they possibly can and ensure they get good answers, specific quantified responses.

Obviously, care takes money, just like anything else. How should a family look at making sure that they have the funds available to go to an assisted living facility, one that has the quality of a Brookdale community? And what are alternative ways to pay for care?

Generally depending on the situation, I think that's where Social Security and annuities or retirement is not enough to cover that. What you find is that you have more and more families that are either looking at a limited amount of savings for retirement benefits that they have, and it only gets them so far. There are other options out there, but they're not foolproof. Some states have some level of assisted programs either through Medicaid or some other branch of social services to provide some assistance. Overall, when it comes to paying for care needs and as care needs advance between a resident using their savings and retirement, we're seeing more companies getting on board to provide additional options with reverse mortgages. You definitely have some of those options, cash-out options on life insurance policies and things of that nature.

But I am so thrilled to see the uptick in long term care insurance. Others will need it far longer than any of the best planning could have foreseen if they don't have some sort of long term retirement or family wealth that's going to sustain decades of advanced care needs.

I'm seeing an increase in awareness, but people have to get more educated and plan better for long term and how they're going to provide for themselves. We've seen a lot of scare with even something that was considered a given: Social Security. People understand we are living longer, and unfortunately we're becoming less and less healthy as we live longer. More of us are going to need longer term but more expensive provision as we age.

What do you see coming for the future of assisted living communities and care for seniors?

I see a lot more tattoos and nose rings, to add comic relief to it. I definitely see that with coming generations, there's a different level of expectation. There's a different level of education, so I think we're going to have far more demanding consumers, both residents that need the services as well as their families to where all companies are going to have to step up and meet the changing needs of the Baby Boomers. Their needs are very different than the previous generation.

I think we're also seeing the younger people coming into the workforce having a much more demanding expectation of what they want in an employer. So maybe work ethic is one way to put it, but we're looking at the fact that we're going to have to have a different model of who's going to be that caregiver 10 years from now. When you look at the fact that our aging population is going to explode over the next couple of decades, the workforce based on projected numbers doesn't look to keep up with that. So I really think that we as a society are going to have to think of some ingenious ways to bring technology and synergies into senior living to maximize the benefit provided for seniors outside of what individual person to person is going to provide. I think that also may be a benefit to people who are living at home, as well. There's going to be a lot of change.

Nursing Home Care

For those individuals that do require round-the-clock care, a nursing home is the best option. A nursing home facility falls under the category of long term health care for patients that need extensive supervision outside of a hospital. Nursing home facilities offer two types of care: the kind that seniors receive when they can no longer perform day to day functions (the ADLs), and medical attention.

The annual cost of a semi-private room in a nursing home facility is just over $80,000, while the cost of a fully private room is a bit more expensive. This cost would total just over $91,000 annually. Unlike independent and assisted living facilities, the costs of nursing homes can be covered through Medicare Part A. The full range of payment options for a nursing home - aside from Medicare - include Medicaid, your private insurance, and the funds you and your family have set aside for any medical emergencies or events.

Spotlight on: Peak Resources

In my never-ending quest to discover all available options to seniors, I had the privilege of sitting down with Kris Thompson, the Executive Director at Peak Resources. We spoke briefly about the services that Peak Resources offers, what families and seniors should look for when choosing a nursing home, and the many benefits awarded to individuals who become a part of this incredible system.

What are your responsibilities as Executive Director at Peak Resources?

I'm pretty much responsible for everything that goes on at the facility. The financial part, the business part, making sure we meet all the rules and regulations, which in healthcare and with nursing homes, there are an awful lot. I'm also involved in the healthcare part of it. There is a director of nursing in the department of nursing that oversees her staff and makes sure that the healthcare aspects of the nursing home are met.

What should a senior look for when choosing a nursing facility? What should the family of the senior look for?

Location. Everyone talks about real estate, which is very important. It's crucial that you're going to feel comfortable visiting, so you want to be close. If you have to drive across town and deal with a lot of traffic, that's probably going to be a burden and a factor that keeps you from visiting. Individuals who enter nursing homes shouldn't lose contact with their family members. I would also recommend that you go through the facility and tour, just do a walk-through. Most facilities would be glad to do that and have a representative walk through with you to answer questions and point out things that the facility offers. As you're walking around, look for common sense things such as this:

▶ Are there any pervasive odors that you notice throughout the facility?

▶ Are the residents of the facility happy? Are they socializing and doing different activities?

▶ Are the staff members happy? If they are happy with their job, that is going to be reflected in their performance and how they interact with residents.

Positive communication is one of the most crucial components that a nursing home resident can have. Is it a warm and welcoming environment? That's always a good thing.

All facilities are also required to have their 25/67, which is their annual survey where the state comes in with nurses, pharmacists, and dietitians. It is state required to make sure that the employees are doing their job. You won't see a federal survey every year, but you're guaranteed that each year the state one will be conducted. They come in and look at all of those rules and regulations, they are making sure that the residents are getting the treatment that they need. They ensure that they are not being taken advantage of and that they can have access to their money right there.

Most facilities have the shopping aspect. On Fridays, we take everyone to the Wal-Mart to go out shopping, and if the resident doesn't feel like going out, he/she can give the list to an employee who is managing the funds to go pick up personal items that the resident needs.

Not all nursing homes are health and rehab facilities, is that correct?

Right, and that's usually part of the Medicare benefits. Most people have Medicaid Part A or Part B. That's going to cover if they're coming in from the hospital. For most people right now, unless it's coming through a bundle payment part of Medicare, you're required to have a three-day hospital stay. You want to make sure that if you are in the hospital, that it is a stay and not an observation because then you are qualified to use your Medicaid Part A benefits. If you meet that criteria - of which therapy or wound care is a part - you can use your Medicaid Part A benefits.

So if you're going to be there at the facility 100 days, that first 20 is covered at 100%. The next 80 days is paid 80%, so there is a 20% co-pay. The supplement would pay that 80% if you have the supplement. Now, if you have long-term care insurance, it would pick up for that deficit and pay. [If you have no supplement or long-term care insurance policy then it is your responsibility to pay from your private funds.]

Does the supplement stop paying if the prognosis of the patient worsens?

Yes. When it comes to the Medicare criteria, the therapist will set up goals, such as, "I want him to be able to walk 10 feet in 5 days". So if the patient is not increasing and making progress - and there's a little bit of leeway there. Some people might have other stuff going on.

They say you can refuse three times, but after that the therapy is going to be required, which is going to drop the Medicare Aid benefits and the supplement, as well.

Say if it's a 10-bed facility, maybe 50% to 80% of the beds are certified, and that can also be with Part A, too. You can have them duly certified with Medicaid and Medicare, or one of each. Of course, if you have Medicare and you're not in the certified bed, Medicare is not going to pay, so the home would advise you of that.

You meet with families from time to time, and you have folks at the facility who are trained to meet with the families to ensure that they have their affairs in order and can find a way to pay for the services and qualify them for the process. Is that right?

Yes, one of the federal regulations is that you have to have a social worker, and with that they do set up systems. You have to have a business manager that takes care of the billing. The social worker will deal with community resources, and there are options there as far as how to help pay or help get them set up in the system. For some families, this is the first time that they are going through the process. Their parents have aged and they have reached that threshold where they need to enter the system. For many, it is a new and unfamiliar process. It can be very complicated, and considering those rules and regulations, they need to know when they meet the qualifications and how to determine eligibility.

Do you find that most families have planned ahead for this type of situation?

No, and I think people tend to put it off and not think that this is going to happen to them. If you look at statistics, you have a one in three chance of being in a skilled nursing facility. A lot has changed now because we do have 20-22% of our residents that are short-term that may come for that Medicare Part A, they get the rehabilitation, and then they're able to go back home to live with their family. Others that return home could receive some type of home health care and sitter. There are a lot of good supports out there.

However, if someone at the facility feels that there is going to be what is known as an unsafe discharge, meaning the individual is well enough to go back home, but perhaps will not be taken care of the way he/she should in the home, then we are required to notify Adult Protective Services (APS). They would come in and do a home assessment to make sure that it is a safe environment for the senior citizen. Someone has to be home to take care of the senior, administer medication, etc. APS checks all of that out, and if they do not like what they see in the assessment, they'll step in. That's not meant to be a big brother system; this is meant to protect the seniors and get their needs met.

If you would like to know more about Peak Resources or speak to one of their employees, you can contact them by phone at 704-482-5396. They are located at 1101 N. Morgan Street in Shelby, NC.

Adult Day Care

One of the more recent options for care is Adult Day Care centers, which are open not only to senior citizens, but individuals who have special needs. I consider myself lucky to be a friend of Suzi Kennedy from the Life Enrichment Center of Shelby, North Carolina. When it comes to taking care of special needs individuals and seniors, Suzi and the people she works with through the Life Enrichment Center have been held up as a national example of how to create a system of adult day care that really and truly works. Not long before publication of this book, I sat down with Suzi to chat about the Center's history and the impact of adult day care in this country. Due to the magnitude of her work, I would be especially honored to dedicate part of this chapter to highlighting what she and the Center have done over the past few decades.

Spotlight on: Life Enrichment Center

The Beginning

Every success story has an interesting background that cannot be ignored. Suzi, originally from New York, moved down South and began teaching nurses aide classes at a community college. When she took her students to the nursing homes to complete the clinical part of her course, she realized something: most of the elderly patients that they encountered were only in these nursing home facilities because they had no other alternative. There was no one to care for them around the clock at home, and in order to ensure they got the attention they needed, their families had entered them into these facilities. This was in the 1970s, meaning back then there were no assisted living homes, according to Suzi. Nursing homes, at least during that time, seemed the only viable option for elder care.

Suzi thought and tried to come up with some alternatives, but at each turn, she was told that her ideas fell under the category of home healthcare, a practice that was already in full swing. She knew that something besides home healthcare could be done, but she didn't know what. Then one night, after watching a television program on nursing homes, she saw an adult day care center in California mentioned in the credits. It was then that it hit her: adult day care was the way to go. This lit a fire in Suzi; she called the California center, collected some information, and later joined a North Carolina state association of adult day care providers. Not long after, Suzi spoke with the minister of John Knox Presbyterian Church here in Shelby, and they opened their doors for the first time as Life Enrichment Center.

Growth and Recognition

1980 was the year that Life Enrichment Center received their first participants: one man and one woman, and they would come to the center twice a week. A year to the day later, however, the Center was logging an average daily attendance of 12 people, which - according to Suzi - in the history of adult day care, that's unheard of. With that level of participation, they opened their doors five days a week and continued to flourish as a not-for-profit organization. In order to have more of an impact on the community, Suzi and the board decided that they would accept different types of funding so that they could serve people who had a variety of funding streams, such as Medicaid. To this day, Suzi swears that was one of the best decisions they ever made, thanks to the enormous positive effect it had on their ability to reach more people in need; not just the elderly, but younger individuals with special needs.

Not long after, the Life Enrichment Center was honored with a $500,000 grant from the Robert Wood Johnson Foundation, and was one of only 16 centers in the United States to receive that recognition. One of the main reasons they were chosen was due to the incredible work that Suzi was doing with Alzheimer's patients. She and a few other people forged the path in the realm of what is known as "behavior acceptance", which is a practice in interacting with Alzheimer's and dementia patients that validates their emotional needs. For instance, Suzi had interacted with elderly patients who were distraught over the loss of their parents. Though their parents had passed away a number of years ago, these patients - due to their illness - were convinced that their parents had just died. Instead of correcting them, which would cause an even greater emotional turmoil, Suzi would sympathize with them and say, "I'm so sorry to hear that. Tell me about your parents." This would greatly comfort the patients, and in a short while, their emotional breakdowns would cease to continue. It was due to this groundbreaking practice that the Robert Wood Johnson Foundation recognized them, and with that newly acquired grant money, they were able to expand even further.

Life Enrichment Center: Today

At the time of publication, the Life Enrichment Center posted the following hours of operation: 5:30 a.m. to 6:00 p.m. This means that families who care for their elderly loved ones can bring them to the center, leave them there if they have to go to work and carry out their responsibilities during the day, and pick them up after work. Individuals who are cared for at the center receive two meals a day, breakfast and lunch, as well as an afternoon snack.

The center also features total healthcare nurses who are available during the hours of operation and can carry out any medical procedure that's approved for the nurses that practice. Individuals at the center can take part in speech, occupational or physical therapy. The center boasts five levels of care, and at the time of publication, the top charge per diem is $68.

To recap on the benefits of this center: families who are caring for a senior citizen or a special needs individual can drop them off at the center in the morning, where they will be taken care of in terms of medical attention, therapy, food, and other activities, and they can be picked up in the evening to go home and eat dinner with their families. This is a tremendously positive option for households that want an alternative to nursing homes and assisted living facilities.

Home Health Care

People are living longer these days. The over-85 age group is the fastest growing population in the United States.Twenty four percent of people over the age of 85 need help with activities in daily living. Some of you have aging parents who may be showing signs of dementia. You might be thinking, can I keep my mom at home? Am I going to have to institutionalize my dad? It's a tough decision. Obviously most people would prefer to stay at home, where they feel most comfortable. Which of us wouldn't rather be at our house and in our own bed? There is also faster recovery in your own home. Infections are less likely as there is no one to get infections from.

Yet if you look up the life expectancy of a family care giver, they often die before the person they're caring for. The reason for that is stress. My beautiful wife and I have six children who depend on us. If I tried to take care of my mother and father on top of that – or my wife did – I couldn't imagine the amount of stress that would put on us. Also, I am simply not trained in that area.

You want to choose an expert that can help with bathing, or running errands or advanced care like providing ventilators. Home care has become very technologically savvy in the last decade. So much can be done in the home that was not possible just a few years ago. This advanced home care enables people to stay at home for much longer than in the past.

Home Health Care: The Wave of the Future?

A good thing to educate yourself on is the types of home health care available to you. Will your home health care situation be the same if you're living in a nursing home, being cared for by a nursing home attendant? You need to ascertain who will be in charge of fulfilling your daily activities, such as going to the grocery store, tidying up the house, preparing meals, and all the basic necessities that need attention.

Types of Care

Many people have arthritis, which according to sufferers is worse in the morning. Once their muscles get warmed up and moving, then they're solid for the rest of the day – but they need help getting to where they can be self-sufficient during the day. These people could be in an institutional setting, or they could stay at home needing one thing to help them get going. Others need help getting ready for bed at night, but during the daytime, they can do their own tasks.

Others have a home health aide ready and available to them 24 hours a day, preparing meals, running the errands, and taking them to the beauty shop. And there are live-in programs as well, someone there to live with the client who might be there 7 days a week, taking responsibility for everything that goes on in the house when the patient can no longer oversee these tasks. These people need someone there with them overnight. If they wake up and need to go to the bathroom in the middle of the night, there's someone to assist them.

Another factor is mere companionship. They want a companion that will sit down with them, read the paper, discuss the news of the day, perhaps watch Jeopardy! and Wheel of Fortune together, talk about it and interact. Skilled nursing is another type of care, where patients who are on a ventilator are given care. These ventilators are only the size of a laptop, but the person can't breathe without it. Taking care of it, suctioning the trachea – that's when you really need someone trained.

Home Health Care Technology

Taking care of someone with a ventilator at home was unheard of years ago. There are so many options for in home care with technology as it is today. Personal emergency response systems or a "Help, I've fallen and can't get up" button – it used to be if you fell down, you pressed the button. But what if you fall down unconscious? Thankfully, modern technology has thought of that. They have reverse engineered the system to detect if a person has fallen. Even if you do not push the button for whatever reason, there is something that will trigger and respond to your fall.

There are also medication-dispensing units, which are actually quite fascinating. Say you need to take your medication at 8:00 in the morning. You first load your medication in the designated cup within a box, and using time sensors, the medication cup will appear at 8:00 on the dot and say, "It's time to take your 8:00 medication." If you do not grab your medication and the sensors announce it three times, then it rings to an operator. The operator will then put a call to your house and say, "You forgot to take your medication". If you do not answer the operator's call, then a phone call is made to your loved ones to come and check on you. The technology in home care is absolutely phenomenal. The military is probably the leader in telehealth. There are programs in the developmental stages right now at various universities that perform cataract surgery on patients in Alaska from Washington via robotic surgery with lasers.

Recently a physician in Paris actually performed an appendectomy on a patient in New York. A doctor was standing by as they were demonstrating it. As we develop that technology more and more, the ability to take care of people in their homes may become the preferred method of administering long-term care.

The point is, everyone wants to stay at home. With these kinds of advances, more people will be able to do that. That's the wave of the future – getting away from centralized hospitals and nursing homes, at least in cases where it makes sense. Obviously there will be a need for those places, but home care is on the low end of the affordability scale and people want to stay at home.

From a Medicare/Medicaid perspective, there are less resources coming out of the system as well. This is a burgeoning, exploding industry with a lot of potential,and regulations with Medicare/Medicaid need to catch up to the wants and needs of seniors.

Advantages of Home Health Care

I believe the number one reason why people prefer to stay at home is because they feel "my home is my castle." It's where people feel comfortable. If I want to walk around in my underwear, I can walk around in my underwear. People recuperate better at home, especially since there is a lower risk of developing an infection in your own home. There is a certain comfort in having that continuity of being home and/or with your loved ones, someone who's familiar with your health problems, mannerisms, and habits. They can pick up on subtle changes quickly, refer them out to the doctor, get them taken care of – whatever they need to have done.

Being cared for in your home is certainly a less dramatic option, and allows you a degree of dignity you may otherwise feel has been taken from you. That's what we're about: trying to help people preserve their hard earned money and property – and keep their dignity in the process.

There are direct health benefits of staying at home, such as less confusion because you are living in a familiar environment, and you are less likely to experience infections, because fewer people live there. Statistics show that people recuperate at home better than they do in an institutional setting.

The majority of people, if given the choice, would rather be at home. Most of the time you don't find people saying, "Please take me out of my home and put me in an institution somewhere. "There are financial benefits to being cared for at home, but the costs of health care in general are high. Unless you have really planned for this with long term care insurance – which is not the norm – you can quickly exhaust your other liquid assets paying for health care, especially as you age.

That's where Medicare and Medicaid come in, whether separately or working in combination. We will get to this concept in a later chapter.

As I have mentioned time and again, preparation is key. It is for this reason you need to ascertain if your loved ones could actually care for you should you decide on home health care. Is your home really a suitable environment for you, one that will meet all your needs?

I will give a more well-rounded glimpse of a successful home health care company that has continued to provide excellent service around the nation in the Spotlight below:

Spotlight On: Bayada Home Health Care

As promised, here is an in-depth look at one of the most successful and reliable Home Health Care companies: Bayada. Some might recognize the name Bayada. This is a nationally-recognized company that sends their people in-home to take care of individuals such as seniors as opposed to sending them to an assisted living or a nursing home. Amber Mitchell, a Client Services Manager for a branch of Bayada, answered some important questions which will be helpful people who are interested in learning more about this topic.

1. What is in-home care?

In-home care can be medical or non-medical services that Bayada can provide to the clients to ensure that while they remain home, they are safe. Bayada is equipped to provide pretty much anything that a hospital or a facility can in the home. It is our mission to keep people in the home, because we know that is where they truly want to be, in the comfort of their own home. Our vision is to help people live safely and comfortably at home with independence and dignity.

2. What are some of the services that Bayada provides?

Bayada provides a range of services to adults and children of all ages to assist with adult nursing and assisted care. The services that are mostly medical include the following:

▶ Rehabilitation services

▶ Hospice (in some areas)

▶ Home health

▶ Physical, occupational, and speech therapy

However, we realize that not every individual might require in-home medical care; some of our clients who are senior citizens simply want someone to help them get up in the morning, get dressed, and be on their way to starting their day. When it comes to services around the house, Bayada is available 24/7 to provide the following:

▶ Bathing and dressing

▶ Administering of medication

▶ Breakfast

▶ Housekeeping, such as laundry and other miscellaneous chores

▶ Errands, such as help with buying groceries

▶ Prescription pick-up

▶ General company (some clients simply want someone to read with them)

In order to determine the best possible care that an individual requires, Bayada will send an agent into the client's home and develop a detailed care plan. These are tailored to the individual to maximize the level of care he/she receives. We have worked the entire gamut, from individuals who want only a few hours of company a day, to people who have required constant, hands-on attention due to having a tracheotomy and being placed on a ventilator.

3. What are the rates, and how are the services paid for?

Normally the standard rate for personal care services is $23/hour. We do have special discounts if you pay privately. We can offer a discount that cuts the rate to $18.25 per hour, which is lower than the national average. There are also other options for payment. We accept Medicaid through the CAP/DA program, we accept the VA Aid & Attendance program, and if you have a long-term policy that will pay for our services, then we accept that as well. We also accept private payment.

When it comes to providing therapy to an individual as part of home health care, Medicare will pay for the physical therapy clients receive during home visits. Those visits are usually a few times a week for an hour or so a day. Medicare will not, however,pay for custodial care, which is where a CNA would go in with the bathing and personal care.

4. Say I have a loved one who is already in a care facility. Can Bayada still work with him/her?

Yes. In that case, two Bayada offices can come in and help provide services: one is the Bayada Home Health Visit Office, located in Gastonia. It is important to note that they service the Gastonia area. They could come in and provide the medical services, such as physical therapy. The second office to become involved would then be our office in Shelby, where we send the CNA out and provide services for bathing and all personal care. So that takes care of the two components: the medical and the custodial.

We currently have several families who have sought our services so that their loved ones do not have to be completely alone in those facilities. We can provide a CNA to sit with them and keep them company for a few hours, and also provide that extra one-on-one care if they should need it.

5. How can people contact you if they want to ask any questions?

Bayada has over 300 locations in the United States, so it is fairly easy to find a location that is close to you. If you'd like to call the Shelby, NC, office, call (704) 669-4000.

Bayada can also send a clinical manager to your home for a sit-down and talk with your family, should the individual seeking care have trouble traveling. You can visit their website at **www.Bayada. com** for further information.

**A Special Thanks to Our Friends at Bayada
Home Healthcare**

I'd like to give a special thanks to my friend Joe Seidel, Division Director at Bayada Home Health Care, and Amber Mitchell, Client Services Manager, for their help with the information in this chapter. The folks over at Bayada really are the best at what they do and have been an invaluable resource for both myself and my clients.

Paying for Home Healthcare

Let's discuss who pays for home health care. Other than having money buried in the backyard or digging into your retirement fund, what are the different options? How can you pay for it? Let's take a look at the average national rates for the various options you have at your disposal:

Nursing Home: about $76,000 per year

Assisted Living: about $40,000 per year

Home healthcare agent: about $21 per hour

You want to plan and be fully prepared to take advantage of at least one of these options, so you can have someone like Bayada Home Healthcare come in and take care of you right in your home. This will avoid you having to be sent to a Medicaid facility or simply left with a Medicaid bed. I encourage you to read up on the different avenues that are available to you in terms of paying for home health care.

Payments and Benefits: Understanding the Differences between Home Health and Home Care

First, let's look at the differences between home health and home care when it comes to insurance. Home health is typically paid for by Medicare. Medicare is a Part A benefit, the home health is a Part

A benefit, so there's no cost for those who have Medicare. If you're over the age of 65, you're home bound and you have Medicare, you can qualify for that program. It covers a 60-day intermittent spell of illness. They pay a bucket of money for the diagnosis that you have. So they will send someone in maybe three days the first week, two days the second week for about an hour for each of those visits, and two days the third week.

By about the fourth week, they're only going to be seeing you about one hour per week. That spell of illness can be renewed, but it typically runs out at 60 days.

Home care, however, is continuous care. They can be in the home anywhere from an hour and a half to 24 hours a day, up to 7 days a week. Those services can be paid for by Medicaid, private insurance, private pay, or VA benefits, to name a few.

Private Funds

One of the first choices is private funds. The individual has the money to pay for it, and so they pay for it. That's obviously going to drain your resources, but is one way home care gets paid for.

Why Long Term Care Insurance Is So Important

Sometimes you're going to look at your insurance policy and it's going to say something about custodial care. A lot of people think, well, I've got this insurance policy that says we get home care.

That is not the definition of custodial care. Custodial care is unskilled services that would be in the home. They're usually talking about home health. Traditional insurances often do not cover continuous care. They mirror what Medicare will pay for, so the home care services are typically not paid for with that.

Long-term care insurance, however, is a viable option and does cover the continuous care that is sometimes needed.

In my assessment of a client's strengths and weaknesses, I routinely recommend that they purchase long-term care insurance. Long-term care insurance has experienced a major overhaul in the last couple of years. There are still traditional long-term care insurance policies. There are also hybrid long-term care insurance policies such as life insurance with long-term care riders and long-term care annuities. In these hybrid long-term care products you may put, for example, $100,000 in a life insurance policy with a long-term care rider. Upon needing long-term care it will begin to pay out maybe as much as four to five times as much as your initial investment in that policy. So you would put in $100,000 which may pay out $400,000 to $500,000 for your long-term care.

Hybrid products, however, generally do not qualify under State Long-Term Care Partnerships for asset protection. Traditional long-term care policies generally do qualify. Let's say you had assets of $100,000 in checking and a traditional long term care policy of $250,000 maximum payout over the term of care which you invested $100,000 in premiums over the years. Even if the policy paid out all $250,000, you would be allowed to keep your $100,000 in checking and still access the long-term care Medicaid system to pay for long-term care under most state long-term care partnerships.

Let's take a look at the criteria needed to be met for long-term care insurance to kick in. A lot of long-term care insurance policies require that you have to have at least two of the activities of daily living (ADL's) being met in order for the policy to be in effect. There are five ADL's of daily living. Bathing, dressing, feeding, toileting, and handling. Then there's assisting with non-personal care. If you hear about the agencies that are non-medical, that's just the meal preparation, light housekeeping, and things of that nature. If you think about the people living at home, that may be the starting point for them. They need someone to come in and maybe help prepare their meal, help them get dressed, or help them bathe.

With long-term care insurance, there's also an elimination period. That is like your deductible. There is usually a 30 to 100-day elimination period, where you have to pay privately during that time. Once you've met that requirement, your insurance policy will kick in and start paying after the elimination period has passed.

Using Medicare or Medicaid to Pay for Home Care

With Medicaid, there are waiver programs. In North Carolina, two Medicaid waiver programs exist for personal care services. One of them is the personal care service, which a physician has to set up. Unfortunately, many physicians are not aware of the program, but we can make sure you get squared away with the proper forms if needed.

The program offers up to 80-hours a month of care, usually over five days a week. So you're getting about two and a half hours a day over those five days. You can get up to 120 hours a month if there's dementia involved. There's also the Community Alternative Program/Disabled Adults (CAP/DA program), that's run by Care Solutions here in Cleveland County, NC. You have to be Medicaid and nursing home eligible to qualify. Typically, people on that program are going to get about 30 to 36 hours a week.

Veterans Administration Benefits

Home Attendant Program:

Another way is through the Veterans Administration (VA), if the person is a veteran. It's called a Home Attendant Program. The way to get the ball rolling is to get your veteran to the local VA and talk with your primary care physician there. Typically, that can give 6 to 9 hours a week of help; that's 2 to 3 days a week of 3 hours of service per day. For those individuals, it may be just what they need to keep them at home. Unfortunately, the hours aren't any longer than that.

This VA program is a great benefit for the veterans who qualify. One of the qualifying factors is you must have served one day in a wartime period, regardless of having been present in the theater of operations. So Korean War, Vietnam War, and Gulf War – if you served one day of service during a wartime period, you may qualify with this program.

The Aid and Attendance Program:

Another payment option is Veterans Administration benefits. The "Aid and Attendance" benefit program through the United States Department of Veterans Affairs. The veteran must have served one day during a war time event or conflict. That doesn't mean they had to be in a battle or on the front lines. The veteran simply must have served one day in the military while the United States was at war. So if you've got a parent that's a veteran, this may be a benefit to look at.

What is the difference in Home Healthcare and Home Care?

As a contrast to home healthcare I sat down with Ruth Huffstetler from Helping Hands Nursing Service, Inc. to talk about the differences between home health and home healthcare as seen in the Spotlight below:

Spotlight on: Helping Hands Nursing Service, Inc.

As part of my continued quest to bring the most varied information out there about Elder Law and elder care, I had the opportunity to speak with Ruth Huffstetler from Helping Hands Nursing Service, Inc. Ruth provided some invaluable facts, figures, and information about what Helping Hands does, as well as what the differences are between home care and home health care.

What are some of the services that Helping Hands offers?

There's no doubt that people want to stay at home. It can be a very traumatic experience for our elders - especially if they are suffering from dementia or Alzheimer's - if they are taken from the surroundings that make them comfortable. Continuity is so important, so by keeping them at home, we're able to stay with them and monitor them. We can go in and make sure that they're not turning on the stove, putting tin foil in the microwave, wandering out in the streets in the middle of the night.

We can also dispense medication. The thing about us is we're doing whatever the family has asked of us. If the family wants us to walk the patient around the house three times at noon for exercise, then that's what we do.

What about nursing services?

Again, if we come to you and your parents are diabetics, and you need them to have certain meds or certain injections as far as their insulin and whatnot, then we help them with those medications or injections. Whatever the family asks of us, we do.

With home health, the doctor is ordering certain physical therapy, occupational therapy, speech therapy. With us, the family is calling and saying, "I've got to go to work, somebody needs to be with Mom and this is what we want done while you're there" or "My mom lives in Shelby but I live in California now. I need 24 hour care and this is what I want done." Sometimes we're truly the only family around because everybody is long distance, and we'll take them up to see the leaves change colors. We'll take them to go visit the old people at the nursing home so they can stay in touch with their friends. We've learned how Chick-fil-A has bingo on certain days and different places we can take them. They can stay involved with their friends.

Can you differentiate between home care and home health care?

The biggest difference in simple terms is that in home health, you have an RN that is supervising everything that's happening. There has been an assessment done and a list of needs that the doctor has ordered. That is home health. They've ordered all the different therapies and there's an RN supervising and making sure those things happen. With home care, you as a family member says, "This is what we need, whether it's someone to be here so we can go see our grandson play football for 4 hours" or "We need 24-hour care". Whatever you want is what you're going to ask us for. That's home care.

Do home health care agencies sometimes refer to you?

Yes they do. Let's say the doctor orders a bath three times a week. They'll have a CNA that's going in on Monday, Wednesday, and Friday giving a bath. There's no set time. It could be at 9 in the morning, it could be 4 in the afternoon. So if the family says, "We need somebody here during the day so we can go to work", those home health agencies will refer to us and say, "Okay, if you call Helping Hands Nursing Service, they can refer someone to you that can be here from 7 in the morning until 5 in the afternoon. They'll be here the whole time to prepare the meals," and then when Home Health comes in to do the therapy or the bath, we let them in, we can assist them, but it's their doing, and then they leave. But we stay.

Do you screen your employees?

First thing is, I have no employees. They are all independent care givers because we are a referral service. Past that, they are all criminal background checked and reference checked. So if you call and say, "I need a caregiver to come out and bathe my mother Monday, Wednesday, and Friday," then we're going to find where you live and what kind of limitations your mom has and we're going to pick who we feel is a good choice based on what you've told us. We'll then refer that person to you. Very important question about the personality: just because I think they're a great choice and I love them dearly, your mother may hate redheads and "I don't want that redhead in my house because she reminds me of my ex son-in-law's wife" or whatever. It doesn't matter. Whatever that case may be, you make a simple phone call and we will send someone else out. You don't have to give us a reason at all because there are personality conflicts with the greatest of people; they just don't see eye to eye.

Do the people you refer provide the transportation or do they take the family's car? Are they paid by the mile if they use the family car?

All of the above. If we take their car, of course there is no fee and we can drive them. If the caregiver uses her own car there is a charge which is just the government rate, I think 0.55 and a half cents now. They do add mileage to their hourly rate.

Do you have written policies for these people or contracts?

What we have is a contract with the caregiver since they are referred and they are actually paying us to keep them working. If they have to call in sick at 3:00 in the morning, they're not calling the family, they're calling me. I make sure someone else is there so you can still go to work. We do have guidelines that we require of them, things that just make me happy as far as what they wear and tattoos not showing, things like that. They are my guidelines. But as far as written rules, it's whatever the family wants. Again, the family may say, "You can take Mom to the beauty shop" and that's all or "Mom's been dying to go see her friend at the VA in Salisbury, would you mind spending a day and taking her there?" And we'll do it. A lot of times the family's car is easier to get in and out of than the caregiver who might drive a big SUV or a little sports car that's hard to get in and out of. So we'll do whatever is best.

How can people pay for home care?

Home care is paid out of pocket or if their long-term policy will allow assignment back to the family, so the family is getting reimbursed for what they have paid. We can assist with that but it is an out-of-pocket. We do not take Medicare, Medicaid, or private health insurance. Insurance might pay for some home health benefits, but they will not pay for the home care.

Hospice Care

Hospice is an amazing organization. Hospice is really a hybrid of in-home healthcare and nursing home care. Hospice care is usually accessed by the patient's family for end-of-life care. Hospice can assist in a range of duties and allows the family to spend the quality time needed with their loved one while Hospice attends to other necessary duties. Hospice also has a number of care facilities where a patient may stay round the clock. I made it a point to seek out an expert on Hospice care for this book and am proud to present Patti McMurray detailing Hospice care in the Spotlight below:

Spotlight on: Hospice

I had the honor of sitting down and talking with Patti McMurry, who has been with Hospice Cleveland County for 25 years. We're going to talk about what it is, any misconceptions, what Hospice does, and the other valuable services to the community.

Tell us a little bit about Hospice Cleveland County, North Carolina.

One thing about our community that we've found is that everywhere we go, no matter if there are conferences, seminars, or anywhere, Cleveland County is very unique because our agencies tend not to compete with each other, but to help each other out. It's a great place to live and raise a family, and then grow old. We took in our first patient 30 years ago, so we're celebrating that. As of today, we have taken care of over 10,000 people who have died in Cleveland County. We were one of the first Hospices in North Carolina.

How did Hospice start?

The word "hospice" actually comes from the Middle Ages. A hospice was originally a resting place for weary travelers. They didn't have hotels, so if people would allow weary travelers to rest in their home, then they would put a lighted candle in their window and that signaled that travelers could stay. When we built our hospice house and our office where we are now, they were going to let us change the name of the road and we thought really hard about what we wanted to name that road. The name is Wendover Heights Drive, and wind needs to go from this place to the next, which is what Hospice does: it helps travelers go from this life to the next life with quality.

It's a pretty new concept; the first Hospice in America was in 1974, so it's very new. Now just about every county in every state in the country has a Hospice. And every country, really, has Hospices. It was similar to the birth experience. Women used to be put to sleep when they had babies: they'd wake up and they'd have a baby. Then, natural childbirth started and things got back to nature, so the concept of death also got that way.

Ninety-five percent of the people who are asked, "How would you like to die?" respond "At home." Much less than half of the people die at home, and everybody wants to yet there are so many things that prohibit that. There's so much fear in that and in modern medicine. We've had people call to set up an admission time, but they're afraid. They're thinking, "If Hospice comes in, Mom's going to die." But think about this: Mom is going to die, we all are. But we want to get in there and make that experience as good as possible. The scary part about Hospice is really only the first 30 minutes of that first visit, and I promise - I tell people this - if we come in for 5 minutes to explain to you what we can do, we will leave in 5 minutes if you want us to. But it's never happened that we've had to leave. People are complimentary and relieved, actually. On the first visit, we give them our 24-hour telephone number that they can call for a nurse to come and visit. Even just having that number, whether they call or not, is so much security to them. You don't have to take somebody to the hospital, you don't have to wonder about anything. We are so involved in patient symptom control, as well.

A large part of the process is not only the death of the patient, but the grief the family members have to endure. How do you include everyone?

A lot of our focus is the family. Hospice is special in that the patient and the family are the unit of care. So the focus is just as much on the individuals of the family as it is on the patient. Oftentimes we'll go in and the patients are doing fine; they know what's coming, they've accepted it, maybe they've struggled and had a lot of treatments, maybe they've suffered a lot and they're really fine. But, for the family members, it's hard to let somebody go. We've had children, we've had young people, and we have very elderly people. So our counselors, chaplains, and social workers really help those families come to terms with those things. Sometimes when we come in, patients are relieved that they can finally say, "I don't want to go to dialysis anymore, I don't want to have another treatment, and I don't want to go back to the hospital." They can say that because they have that support, they know that those team members are going to be there to help the family.

How is Hospice funded? How does one pay for Hospice care?

This is something I think the public does not realize: when you are a Hospice patient, Medicare has a benefit called a Hospice benefit for in home care. That benefit pays for everything that Hospice does. It pays for the staff, it pays for the equipment that has to be rented, it pays for oxygen, it pays for any supplies. It's the benefit that kicks in before the supplement, which also covers 100% of all the medications that the patient is taking. So sometimes we can get in there and save patients and families thousands of dollars a month, because anything pertaining to that illness - heart disease, which is our primary diagnosis, or anything else you may have that you need medication for - is paid for 100%, even if it's over the counter. A lot of people don't know that. The only criteria to be a Hospice patient is the doctor feels like if the illness follows its normal course, that the patient will live 6 months or less. Now, we've had patients for a lot longer than that, but our median length of stay is 11 days. That means 50% of our patients die within 11 days after we admit them. So they're not able to access that Medicare benefit and get all those things paid for. That is the one thing about Hospice care that keeps me awake at night, is knowing that there are so many people who could benefit from having that support of the staff that they can call, but also financially. Being sick is very expensive.

We're very proud of the work we do and the relationships we've forged with the patients. We've named the rooms in honor of the people who we've cared for, so it's a complement to our staff and the patients that have worked together.

CHAPTER 4

A Special Word on Dementia and Alzheimer's

As elder law attorneys we are specially situated to find solutions to many of the problems these conditions bring with them. While we have yet to find a cure to stop dementia, we can help protect those in its clutches while the medical world continues to tackle prevention, treatment and reversal of the conditions.

Dementia Defined

The Alzheimer's Association defines dementia as, "a general term for a decline in mental ability severe enough to interfere with daily life. Memory loss is an example. Alzheimer's is the most common type of dementia."

Dementia is not actually a specified disease. It describes instead, a general decline in memory or other thinking skills and is identified through a variety of symptoms. Alzheimer's disease accounts for 60% to 80% of dementia cases. To be characterized as dementia, at least two of the following mental functions must be significantly impaired: visual perception; reasoning and judgment; memory; communication and language; or ability to focus and pay attention.

Dementia is not a normal part of aging as the terms "senility" or "senile dementia" infer. If a loved one is having trouble with any two or more of these mental functions, it's a good idea to get it checked by an expert. Dementia is progressive and takes over the mental functions over time. In this way, it provides the individual and the family, time to plan for its disastrous effects[6].

Cost to the Individual

The cost to the individual with dementia is difficult to quantify. Because dementia is a progressive condition and one where aging is the greatest risk factor, it is logical that at the beginning and earlier stages of dementia, the cost to the individual is minimal. As dementia progresses, so does the need for assistance with daily activities. This often comes in the form of meal preparation, help with grooming and hygiene, transportation, and help with many other daily activities. Dementia patients can become so mentally challenged that they may place themselves in dangerous situations, such as walking neighborhoods and getting lost. While the individual affected by dementia may need only a few hours of help per week when the symptoms first manifest, they may soon need 24-hour supervision, not only for assistance with daily activities, but to protect them from themselves. The individual's costs will include medical expenses and paying for a caregiver.

Caregiving for one with dementia varies depending on the quantity of care required. An in-home caregiver may charge $21 per hour or higher. Adult day care can run as high as $18,200 per year or more. When an individual can no longer live alone but is not ready for a nursing home, Assisted Living facilities are available but may cost as much as $42,600 per year or more. When around the clock care is needed, a nursing home can cost an individual up to $90,520 per year, or higher. To view costs in other states and national average costs of long term care, see the MetLife Survey of Long Term Care Costs[7].

[6] http://www.alz.org/what-is-dementia.asp
[7] https://www.metlife.com/mmi/research/2012-market-survey-long-term-care-costs.html#keyfindings

Cost to the Family

Where the individual with dementia is fortunate enough to have family nearby, the family will often step up to help a loved one with their daily activities. Again, the process can be gradual and before the helpful family member realizes it, they find themselves missing work and then quitting their job to give proper care to the dementia patient. The cost to the family includes the loss of income from this family member's job.

The less recognizable cost to the family is the emotional strain placed on the family member caregiver. To save the family money, many family members will work nearly twenty-four hours a day, seven days per week. The ramifications are physical, mental and emotional health problems to the caregiver and surrounding family members. The medical costs and possible future psychological costs to the caregiver, must be considered.

It is important for family members to take a step back and assess this cost. Providing a caregiver with time off every day, week and year helps maintain the caregiver's health. The caregiver must have support to keep caring for their loved one.

Cost to the Nation

As a nation we have begun to recognize the devastation that dementia has caused and will continue to cause. Organizations such as the Alzheimer's Association have been effective in lobbying for monies to be put towards the research of dementia treatment, prevention and reversal. The cost of dementia to our nation has been a great motivator for politicians to fund such research. A study conducted by RAND Corporation in 2013, estimated the national cost of dementia to be between $159 billion to $215 billion (including an estimate for the monetary value of informal care provided)[8]. The majority of the costs associated with dementia are for institutional and home-based, long-term care, and not medical services.

[8]http://www.rand.org/news/press/2013/04/03.html

Medicare and Medicaid pay for some of this cost, which amounts to a taxpayer burden. According to the Alzheimer's Association March 2013 Fact Sheet, it's estimated that Medicare and Medicaid paid approximately $142 billion in caring for those with Alzheimer's or other dementia's[9]. It is in the best interest of the nation's economy to continue research on prevention, treatment and reversal of these conditions.

Concluding Thoughts on Dementia and Alzheimer's

The costs of dementia can devastate the affected individual, their family and the nation. While scientists continue to search for solutions to the debilitating condition, families affected by it must face its challenges. It is recommended that those families seek emotional support by way of a therapist or support group. In addition, finding an elder law attorney can benefit the affected individual and family members in several ways. Elder law attorneys can guide families to important resources available for the financial and other challenges they will face. Elder law attorneys can also make sure the family's assets are being used in the most efficient manner considering other available resources and the family's individual goals.

Spotlight on: Teepa Snow, Expert on Dementia and Alzheimer's

For this interview, I was honored to be able to connect with expert in Alzheimer's and dementia, Teepa Snow. During our discussion, Teepa and I spoke about everything from care to causes and what needs to change in the systems to allow for more humane treatment of loved ones with Alzheimer's and dementia.

How did you come to be the expert's expert in Alzheimer's and Dementia?

It's interesting, I would have never thought that. But I started off doing a lot of work with the USD [University of San Diego] School of Medicine and I was part of a team when I graduated and got my

Occupational Therapy degree. I have worked in long-term care, so when they were looking for somebody it seemed like a good match, and I had the good fortune to work with a good nurse, a good social worker, and then a couple of really good, strong family practicing general internal medicine physicians who understood geriatrics really well. That allowed me to learn the art of working with lots of disciplines, but to work with people that have dementia.

Then I did some work with head injury, and I did that for three years. I also went back and worked again with dementia in a psychiatric setting. Then I did home care and community care, and I worked at the VA. During all this time I kept building expertise in geriatrics and I find more and more I understood dementia and could work with those with dementia and show improvement while working with their caregivers a lot better than most of my colleagues. I found it interesting and exciting, not scary and awful. During that time I'd also be doing in-services and training, so as time went by people would start going with me to do things. Then I worked for the Alzheimer's Association as the Education Director in the eastern North Carolina area. We made a couple of training videos because we were doing workshops, which led people to want more and more workshops. So we thought, "Okay, let's develop a video now." The video became the video used nationally by many groups that addressed the issues one would face when trying to care for someone with dementia. From there it snowballed.

What would you say has been your experience with patients with Alzheimer's and Dementia? And what is the difference between the two?

That is the most common question I am asked. Think about dementia as a great big umbrella, and under that umbrella, one of the boxes is Alzheimer's disease. But there's other boxes: there's frontal temporal lobe dementia, there's alcohol-related dementia. So we've got a lot under that umbrella, but if it is under the umbrella it means four things: 1.) that at least two parts of the brain are starting to die, and what's causing it will vary. 2.) as of right now, if it truly is dementia, there is nothing we can do to slow it, stop it, or turn it around. We don't have anything to get rid of it; none of the drugs change the disease. 3.) if it's truly dementia, it's going to get worse, it's going to progress. All sorts of dementia are neuro-degenerative, meaning they kill off the nerve cells in the brain. 4.) they're all terminal illnesses, and once you have it, if nothing else kills you first then it will kill you. It will destroy so much of your brain that your brain can't run your body anymore. So if you make it to the end, you'll die of pneumonia because you can't coordinate your swallowing and your breathing and your ability to fight infection. So you'll get an infection in the blood stream that you can't fight. If you get dehydrated and your brain says, "You don't need any fluid," your brain then says that you're done.

We didn't used to keep track of that as dementia, but it's actually the dementia that's causing your body to shut down. And now it's the 5th leading cause of death for people over 65 and the 11th leading cause of death for all ages.

And the only one we don't have a cure or treatment for.

That's right, nothing that does anything for the disease. The only thing we have is that some people benefit from some of the medications some of the time for a short period of time. That's it. That's all we have. Care, therefore, becomes the critical feature, and yet if we look at our care patterns and what the government support is, it's nothing. We do nothing for people living with dementia, we manage their acute medical illnesses poorly because primarily we don't know what to do with dementia but I can fix the UTI. So what I'll do is tie you down and give you antibiotics. Well, what's going to happen the next time? We'll do it again and again, but where are we going with that? So we unfortunately put people through a lot of distress because no one really understands what the disease looks like. Doctors think, "I can treat that" but yet they can't treat the dementia.

Does a living will help in these situations in any way?

Well, let's say I have an advanced directive that with any other health condition would be honored. The only state in the nation right now if I developed dementia would be Oregon. In every other state, dementia precludes me from having my directive followed.

You unveil an important point, which is the living wills apply to when someone is terminally incurable, brain death has occurred

and they're being maintained by respirators. That doesn't count for this situation where the mind is not coordinating with the body.

This idea of competence is really complicated when it comes to dementia; because although I may not be competent to handle financial affairs, I might be competent to decide whether or not I want turkey or chicken for dinner. But that's not how we've divided the pie here; it's all black and white.

So the legislature needs to work with people like you that are on the front lines in developing laws and directives to account for situations like Dementia and Alzheimer's.

Yes, because they don't exist. With feeding tubes, they came to the realization that actually we weren't improving anybody's life and the value of doing that was actually nil. It actually didn't change the quality or quantity of life, it made people more likely to have bad things happen.

You deal in the healthcare industry on a regular basis. How much abuse of those directives is present?

It's possible, but let's figure out what's going on, and I would think the abuse that goes on to the people who have dementia is much worse right now because they are put through things that I don't know how anyone can do to another human being. And they call it "care".

I've said before, we treat animals in end of life situations better than people.

Right, where is that going to take somebody? And to get people to take that step back and go, "Guys, this is not euthanasia like you're talking about. I'm not taking somebody's life away from them, I'm helping them do the things that they really value." And yet we are more than willing to restrain people, tie them up, give them additional medications to make them protest so that I can deliver the "treatment" I believe they should have so they can live three more days.

With zero quality of life and lots of pain. That's ridiculous.

How many times are we going to put somebody through this before we say, "You know, they said no." Okay, let's get people together and work through this before we get to this place so that we're really acting in the person's best interest. Not working from anyone's opinion, but what the patient clearly asked for before this started.

This is going to be a movement from the ground up. I think Wisconsin and Minnesota are dealing with the issues, and they're dealing with the issues because they, like North Carolina, have a large rural aging population. The resources are changing, the care situations are problematic. And people would rather die on their farm than move into a facility and lose their sense of identity and purpose. So how are we going to deal with this? Something needs to change about how care is delivered; people would never choose that. You walk into these places and you go, "Yes, better than it used to be," but would I live here? Absolutely not.

People pay phenomenal sums of money for an intensive care stay at the end of life for no decent outcome whatsoever, no quality of life during the process. And yet we will not pay a penny for the person to be cared for in a different situation.

With 2/3 of the population being over 65 since 2010, Dementia and Alzheimer's on the rise, you have to be able to identify it and then know how to react to it to give proper medical care.

And yet there is no requirement at all for hospitals to have any kind of training in dementia, for EMS services to have any kind of specific training in dementia or police and fire departments, yet they're the front lines, they're the people out there in the community.

The civil rights issue for people living with dementia is finding that balance between what support and care I do need, and people making decisions about me without me, and me being able to be incarcerated for the rest of my life without a trial. If you put me in a secure unit, I may never get out again. Who's to say that I'm there by virtue of what's best for me versus what's best for my oldest son who decided that I was causing a lot of trouble and it would be easier for him to manage my estate without me being present?

Right now across North Carolina, it is permissible to lock people up and it doesn't matter what they want or what they think. It's rampant and it's a knee-jerk reaction. At a national level, the conversation is happening regularly. Yet nobody wants to address this because you'd actually have to address this.

That leaves a good question on the civil rights issue: who's going to fight that issue, and how do you fight that issue when you really don't have a client that's competent to be had?

What I think we're going to see is more and more younger onset patients say, "No, you're not going to put me here." And what happens is they typically get kicked out to the psyche unit and back because they get in trouble. So people are not sure what to do with the young onset people, and I think some will end up being lawyers and judges and someone is going to say, "I'll take you to court." I think we're getting to that point where there are enough higher profile people who are getting this condition who are smart people, and they're going, "Wait a minute, you can't just do this to me." And up until now there's been just a few of them, but I think the numbers are starting to rise a little bit.

Has this [Dementia and Alzheimer's] always existed throughout time with humanity? Or is this something new? It seems like this wasn't the case when I was little; it was senility. But were we just calling it something else?

Some of it has been around but not the amount and not the intensity. Our lifestyle is dramatically changing and our environment is changing, not only the environment of the brain but our environment and how we live our lives is very different than it was a generation and a half ago. I think when you start doing that over time, what we're finding is high stress, sleep deprivation, and high sugar intake with limited opportunities to socialize and engage leads to certain types of dementia in that umbrella. Certain types have become much more prevalent than what we used to see. We never saw it like we're seeing it now. We're also seeing more young onset situations. So I think we have lots of different things happening, but now we're seeing an increased number of survivors who live long enough to whom the things that wouldn't have happened because they were gone, are now happening. If you look at many of the young onset folks, you're going to see the high intensity people, and they worked really hard to the point where they never gave themselves a break. We know that with people who are high-risk worriers - worrying is a bad habit because you can't let it go - the risk goes up.

It's been a pleasure to interview you. Thank you

It was a pleasure to interview such an expert as Teepa Snow. We really got into this discussion and went down many twists, turns and winding roads related to dementia and Alzheimer's. Even after reading this interview multiple times I find myself emotionally stirred, wanting to help, wanting to fix things. I feel helpless that I can't fix the many problems with treatments, cures or policies that affect someone suffering from these afflictions. What I can do, however, is to help families think and plan ahead. To put in place healthcare directives and powers of attorneys to appoint trusted decision makers for the afflicted. I can assist a family in protecting assets while offering healthcare options. I can lobby our politicians for more flexible tools and regulations that govern how we treat our loved ones who are suffering. I cannot change these things alone. Teepa cannot change these things alone. Together change can occur and we can help people with dementia or Alzheimer's to live and die with dignity and by their rules.

CHAPTER 5

Senior Dental Care

By now, there have been a variety of terms that have been used throughout this book that refer to the health, well-being, and the overall care that all seniors deserve to receive. Many of you reading this might be sons and daughters eager to ensure the best care is delivered to your mother and father. Yet certain aspects of healthcare when it comes to taking care of Mom and Dad, or Grandma and Grandpa tend to be overlooked. For this reason, the focus of this chapter will be Senior Dental Care.

It's no secret - a fact confirmed in an interview appearing in this section – that the function of our bodily organs is linked in certain respects to the quality of our dental health. Poor dental health can be detrimental to anyone, though the risks involved increase drammatically if the individual is elderly.

Academic literature paints a dismal picture of the state of Senior Dental Care in the United States and around the world. That is why it's crucial to keep dental health in mind when we speak about overall senior healthcare. If left by the wayside, dire consequences will follow.

Impact on Health and Well-Being

According to an article published by the *Clinical Interventions in Aging* journal, problems that occur with a senior's dental health "were found to be correlated with worse quality of life."[10] The study conducted sought to examine first the major dental issues that are impacting the elderly community, and second, the ramifications of letting these issues go ignored or delayed in their treatment. Cavities rank as one of the top issues facing Senior Dental health around the globe. If a cavity goes unchecked, it could lead to tooth decay; the longer it goes untreated, the more the tooth will rot until it has to be removed. If detected early, dentists will remove only the decayed part of the tooth, and use a fluoride treatment to restore the remaining tooth, rather than removing it altogether and replacing it.

The second problem posed to Senior Dental Health is what the article labels "accumulation of bacterial plaque", which we know can be the result from either not brushing our teeth, or not brushing them correctly. The accumulation of this if unaddressed, leads to periodontal disease. The more severe this disease, the more the need to have the tooth removed.

Dry mouth can be a side effect to taking certain medications, and is another problem the article explored. Severe dry mouth can lead to certain oral disorders in extreme cases - such as fungal infections of the mouth - and overall can be a painful malady to cope with on a day-to-day basis. While treatments can be prescribed to seniors diagnosed with moderate to severe dry mouth, few are successful, increasing the need for good preventative dental care.

Oral cancer was the last issue profiled in the article, and is said to include "lip, oral cavity, and pharyngeal cancer—the eighth most common cancer worldwide". Once diagnosed with oral cancer, the patient may suffer from "major anatomical changes in the oral cavity"

[10] "Oral health in the elderly patient and its impact on general well-being: A nonsystematic review". CIA Clinical Interventions in Aging. 2015

that affect everyday functions such as "speaking, chewing, and/or swallowing", making day-to-day activities extremely difficult for the elderly.

One element that the article includes in addition to the health impacts of poor dental care, is the social impact on the elderly. Senior patients suffering from any of the above maladies and disorders will likely feel their social lives are compromised. They can feel self-conscious from the difficulty of performing simple communicative and food-related tasks. Senior Dental health therefore affects how seniors speak and how and what they eat, taking not just a physical but a mental toll on them.

Edentulism and Nutrition

Edentulism is the medical term for being without teeth. In the upcoming interview, the number of natural teeth a senior has is directly linked to his or her longevity, and the research proves why.

In another study published by the *International Journal of Dentistry*, edentulism is a negative phenomenon that weakens an individual's ability to chew: "Most studies agree that denture wearers have only about one-fifth to one-fourth the bite strength and masticatory force of dentate individuals." This means those who wear dentures cannot bite or chew food with as much strength as the individuals who have their natural teeth. "Furthermore, complete denture wearers require 7 times more chewing strokes than those with natural dentitions to be able to cut food into half of its original size". So not only are they unable to chew with as much strength, *they have to chew more* to properly swallow and digest their food. This in turn affects the food choices they make; whereas once seniors cooked or ordered anything they desired, when edentulism sets in, they are forced to eat softer foods. These softer foods might not provide the nutritional value tougher foods provide, e.g. protein from meat.

In fact, the journal published a long list of the effects on an individual's overall health as a result of edentulism. Some of these effects are reproduced below[11]:

▶ Lower intake of fruits and vegetables, fiber, and carotene and increased cholesterol and saturated fats, in addition to a higher prevalence of obesity, can increase the risk of cardiovascular diseases and gastrointestinal disorders.

▶ Decreased daily function, physical activity, and physical domains of health-related quality of life.

▶ Increased risk of chronic kidney disease.

▶ Association between edentulism and sleep-disordered breathing, including obstructive sleep apnea.

Both articles suggest the effects of poor dental hygiene and edentulism impact not only general health, but the social and the emotional well-being of the individual diagnosed with oral disorders. There are many elements to elder law and senior care that I promote; preventative dental care is absolutely one of them. With so much research supporting a link between good oral health and longevity, I urge you - if you're a senior - to take preventative care. Even if you're not a senior, the signs are clear; take care of your teeth. It's that simple. It will not only save you from developing disease, it will save you time, money, and your mental well-being later on.

Spotlight on: Senior Dental Care

I'm very proud to have met with Kendalyn Lutz-Craver from Cornerstone Dentistry in Shelby, NC. There's a huge need in the community for proper senior dental care. There's a hole in the Medicare/Medicaid system to pay for proper dental care for seniors, and many times seniors will either put off care or not receive proper care when they need it. There's proof of a connection between longevity and dental care. So it's an issue that's germane to seniors and is certainly something that needs to be addressed. Therefore, Kendalyn and I have been discussing ways to work on some of these issues. I wanted to bring those thoughts to you.

Cornerstone Dental Associates is a pretty amazing facility.

Thank you, we're very proud of it. We've been in there 6 years now, and it's the first green building in the county. We were really thoughtful about the process and wanted to take something that's not fun for anyone - dentistry - and make it a more comfortable environment, an environment where you're excited to come get care and you feel like you're a part of the family.

It's the first green building in the county?

Yes, a few patients did ask me if we were going to actually paint the building green. But this means that it is LEED certified, LEED referring to Leadership in Energy and Environmental Design and so it's a point system. You work with the architect, you work with the contractor and you achieve different points to get your certification. We recycled about 75% of our construction waste. Every employee is guarantee a daylight view. We do things that reduce the chemicals that come off the paints and furniture. The fresh air comes in, so that exchange is permitted. You just do a series of things to make it a positive work environment, and a lot of research has shown that with green buildings, you produce healthier employees as well. There are less sick days.

What made you want to be a dentist?

I was part of that small percentage of people that always loved going to the dentist; it was always fun for me, I had a great dentist growing up. Teeth are very important. If you ask people what they notice when they first meet people, eyes and teeth seem to be the two that come up. And it changes the demeanor of someone if they don't have confidence in their teeth. You see it tremendously. As for my journey, I grew older and figured out what I liked in school. I loved math, I loved science and then thought about what my goals were into adulthood and that I loved the idea of having a career where I could be my own boss. And I could use the math and science that I like, but also have some flexibility of schedule. It was important to me to have a work-life balance, to be able to be a mom as well as a dentist.

What do you do when you see a senior?

We start every patient with what we call an initial exam, and it's a long appointment. You're going to hang out with me and my assistant for an hour and a half. We're going to take any needed X-rays and photos, and we're just going to talk about the goals you have and figure out the needs you have, the best way to tackle them, and how to make them affordable for you. A lot of patients are surprised when they call our offices because they think, "Well I just need to come in and get a cleaning." But what people don't realize is there are different types of cleanings based on your needs and it's crazy to jump in before we know what's going on. I love that chance to get to know the patient and for the patient to start to get to know me, to build a good relationship with me. I want patients that are comfortable asking questions any time. So we start there.

Sadly, dental insurance is not like health insurance, so more than anything we think of it as a benefit. And in this day and time, it's a benefit some people get with employment. I don't know if there's any anymore that get dental benefits after they retire. So we offer lots of payment plans, lots of ways to make it affordable, and we try to work with our patients once they hit the age of about 50-55, until 65 or whenever the retirement horizon is to get their mouth ready for retirement, ready for the time when hopefully they just need maintenance. It's very much like pre-planning.

For instance, if you had big fillings and we need to transition them to crowns, we're looking at what we have to do over the next five to ten years. Doing it all at once would be overwhelming and extremely expensive, so we break it down; we do a little bit at a time to step patients along. Many seniors are on a fixed income, so the biggest message to get out to patients first and foremost is: Just because you don't have dental insurance doesn't mean that dentistry is not available, that it's so far out of reach that sometimes we have a tendency to equate dental costs with health costs. Dentistry doesn't have the same cost as one would have with health care; it is an investment. It's not cheap by any means but it is not prohibitive if you do not have dental insurance.

So it's a misconception to think if you don't have dental insurance, you can't afford dental work?

Yes. We figure out first everything you need. If you only need two hygiene visits a year with diagnostic X-rays, we have some patients that pay that and divide it up into twelve payments. They make a payment every month if they want a small payment. Others choose to pre-pay before their visit, if you pre-pay you get a 5% discount. Some divide it every three months. There are lots of different ways to do it.

What about longevity? I've always wondered if there's a connection between longevity and dental care, and I understand that there is. Is that right?

There definitely is. Twenty is our magic number. At the office, we do a party every year to celebrate all of our patients, 80 years or older, with 20 or more of their natural teeth. But all the research shows that 20 teeth have to function together. So 10 top and 10 bottom lined up. If you have 20 or more, you're going to function well, it's going to improve longevity; less than 20, we see an increase in mortality rate. So as you begin to lose teeth and pass that tipping point, your life expectancy decreases. That's big. Keep as many of your natural teeth as you can.

What about gum care?

Gum care is huge, and a lot of people are becoming more familiar with that, but periodontal disease - this is an inflammatory process, caused by bacteria. That leads to chronic inflammation, bacterial issues, diabetes, and cardiovascular disease. Some studies now are looking at dementia. It's all linked. But it makes sense, and if we stop and think about it, sometimes we think about our mouth as a completely different part of our body. It's not; it's where everything starts. And so it has a huge systemic impact, and that comes into hygiene care. It is so important to keep your gums healthy.

The other thing we like to work with patients: I'm a huge proponent of electric toothbrushes, but especially as we get older because if you think about a small toothbrush, you need good dexterity and you need a good grip for a small, narrow toothbrush. But a nice big toothbrush, we love Sonicare, it does better than anything we can do. I love to get patients with an electric toothbrush. We also have patients who are on medications, and what's a side effect of those medications? Dry mouth. Dry mouth leads to increased cavities, and it all cycles. So when you come, throw in a fluoride treatment with your hygiene visit and then do fluoride rinses at home. We also like to look at diet. Sadly, we're a country of a lot of diabetics and obese people; a lot of that comes from poor diet choices such as soft drinks, sports drinks - sugar or sugar free, because a lot of that is the acidic component. Once you get dry mouth, you want to keep your mouth wet so we start grabbing candies to suck on. So it's thinking about all those things. If you're going to keep them, you've got to get smart about it.

Everything has to do with longevity. Once you begin to lose teeth, you start to chew with less efficiency. And when it comes to dentures, you're affected there as well. Not only do the bones shrink, but your jaw muscles begin to atrophy because you can't apply nearly the biting force onto a denture that you can with your natural teeth. So for anyone with dentures who wants to chew a good steak, they have to chew seven times more than someone without dentures because of the decreased force. All that adds up. You don't have as many teeth, it's hard for you to chew, and what do you do? You start eating more processed foods, and everything just devolves. That's a lot of the increased mortality, losing teeth.

If you look at the history of dentistry in this country, you realize how crucial it is. By letting a toothache go on and on for whatever reason, you are increasing your risk of major physical, emotional, and social issues, and affecting your self-confidence and self-esteem. Dental care is not something you want to ignore. It is extremely important to your overall health and in fact your longevity.

CHAPTER 6

Medicaid Crisis Planning: How to Plan for a Medicaid Crisis

You should be well aware by now that planning and preparation are my mantras, but in the event of a Medicaid crisis, will you know the first steps to take? What will you do to fix the problem and avoid the crisis from happening in the first place? Before we discuss the "how" and the "why", let's first get a few things straight.

The Difference Between Medicare and Medicaid

Medicare and Medicaid are totally separate programs, but how do they differ? The application periods are different and when to apply may also be different. In a long-term care crisis how long does Medicaid pay for care? When does Medicaid pay for care? These and other questions will be explored in this chapter.

Medicare is basically a health benefit for people who are typically over 65 years of age. If you are under 65 and have a disability lasting longer than 2 years, you can qualify for Medicare prior to age 65.

Medicaid however, is really designed for the indigent, for those who don't have the financial means to care for themselves. Carved out of that is a health care program and typically they fall under Medicaid waivers. But Medicaid and other benefit programs do differ from state-to-state.

The following article on the Medicaid systems for long-term and other care was written by attorney Elizabeth Dickey for the NOLO website.

When Medicaid in North Carolina Will Pay for Long-Term Care in a Nursing Home

North Carolina's Medicaid program will pay for a nursing home only if you have limited income and assets and you need skilled nursing.

In North Carolina, Medicaid is a common source of funding for long-term care, particularly when people have already used up all of their own assets to pay for private care. And this doesn't take long -- in 2012, the average daily cost of a private room in a nursing home in North Carolina was $228. Plus, private health insurance policies generally do not cover long term care, very few people purchase private long-term care insurance policies, and Medicare coverage for long-term care services is very limited.

In North Carolina, Medicaid is administered by the Division of Medical Assistance (DMA). To apply for Medicaid, contact the Department of Social Services office in your county. You can also apply online.

Not everyone can get Medicaid to pay for nursing home care in North Carolina, however. You must medically require skilled nursing care, and your income and assets must fall under the state Medicaid limits. The eligibility rules for long-term care services like nursing homes are different than for other Medicaid services.

When a Nursing Home Is Considered Medically Necessary in North Carolina

Medicaid will pay for a nursing home only when it is medically necessary. You must show that you "meet the nursing facility level of care," meaning that you need the kind of care that can only be provided in a nursing home.

To show that you meet a nursing home level of care, you must show that your physician thinks you need the kind of services that are only offered in a skilled nursing facility. For example, you can meet the nursing facility level of care by showing that you need the services of a registered nurse for several hours a day, or by showing that you need daily assessments of your condition by a licensed nurse, or by showing that you need medication administered frequently by a nurse. If you have a nasogastric tube, require dialysis, frequent injections, or respiratory therapy, you are more likely to meet the nursing facility level of care.

If you need only custodial care such as help with activities of daily living (bathing, dressing, eating, getting in or out of a bed or chair, and using the bathroom), you are not likely to meet the nursing home level of care. (In this case, you may want to read the second part of this article on when North Carolina Medicaid will pay for assisted living or home health care.)

North Carolina's Medicaid Income Limit

People who receive SSI already qualify to receive Medicaid long-term care in North Carolina. If you don't receive SSI, and you are 65 or older, blind, or disabled, you must have income below $973/month for a household of one or $1,311/month for a household of two (in 2014).

If your income is above the limit, you still might be able to qualify for Medicaid if you have medical expenses that meet or exceed the amount of extra income you have. The Division of Medical Assistance (DMA) will calculate how much your monthly income exceeds the Medicaid income limit and then will multiply that amount by six. This amount is your Medicaid deductible. Once you satisfy your deductible, you are eligible for Medicaid for a period of six months. After six months, DMA will assess another deductible.

You can satisfy your deductible by showing DMA that you have medical expenses, including nursing home charges, that equal or exceed your deductible. You do not have to pay medical bills for them to count towards your deductible; you just need to show proof that you incurred the expenses. Because nursing homes are so expensive, the Medicaid deductible is a common way for nursing home residents to become eligible for Medicaid.

North Carolina's Medicaid Resource Limit

To qualify for Medicaid in North Carolina, you must have no more than $2,000 in resources (assets like money and property). Some property does not count toward the resource limit. In North Carolina, your home is exempt up to an equity value of $543,000, as long as you intend to return there or if your spouse or another dependent relative lives there. In addition, one car is exempt if it is used for transportation for yourself, your spouse, or a dependent relative. Personal belongings and household goods are also exempt. Retirement accounts are counted as assets to the extent you can withdraw money from them.

Spousal Maintenance Allowance in North Carolina

If you have a spouse who is going to continue to live independently while you go to a nursing home, then North Carolina will allow you and your spouse to keep more income and assets to support that spouse.

Income. First, your spouse (called the "community spouse") may be allowed to keep some of your income each month. The amount that DMA determines that your spouse can keep will depend on how much separate income your spouse has and also how much he or she spends on housing. In 2014, the minimum monthly "community spouse income allowance" is $1,967, and the maximum is $2,931.

In addition, if you have dependents who will remain in the community while you go to a nursing home, these dependents might be entitled to keep some of your income. This is called the dependent family member allowance. Your dependents must be claimed as dependents on your tax return to qualify for this allowance. The amount your dependent can keep from your income depends on whether they have income of their own. The maximum that a dependent can keep is $656/month.

The amounts that DMA calculates for your community spouse's income allowance and your dependents' family member allowance reduce the amount of your Medicaid deductible. So, if you have a spouse receiving $2,931 and a dependent receiving $656 (for a total of $3,587 per month), then your six month Medicaid deductible is reduced by $21,522 ($3,587/month for six months).

Assets. North Carolina assumes that half of the assets that you had at the time of your first admission to a nursing home (called the "community spouse resource allowance," or CSRA) belong to your spouse, subject to a limit that changes annually. The limit for the CSRA in 2014 is $117,240 [$119,220 in 2016]. The minimum is $23,448. When you apply for Medicaid, DMA will tell you how much your community spouse is entitled to keep. If your spouse needs more, you can go to court and ask a judge to allow a higher CSRA.

When you apply for Medicaid, your CSRA is subtracted from your countable assets at the time of your application. For example, say Mr. Brown has $80,000 in countable assets when Mr. Brown moves into a nursing home on February 1st. Mrs. Brown continues to live in the couple's home. Mr. Brown uses half of his savings to pay for his nursing home care until December 1st, when he applies for Medicaid. On December 1st, Mr. Brown has $40,000 in countable assets. Because Mrs. Brown's CSRA is $40,000, she is entitled to keep the $40,000. Mr. Brown then has no countable assets, and he meets the resource eligibility criteria for Medicaid.

Personal Needs Allowance in North Carolina

If you receive Medicaid and live in a nursing home, you will be expected to spend almost all of your income on your care. North Carolina allows nursing home residents receiving Medicaid to keep just $46/month as a personal needs allowance.

Read on to find out about when Medicaid will pay for assisted living or home health care in North Carolina.

North Carolina's main Medicaid program does not pay for assisted living facilities or home health care as it does for nursing home care, but it offers a few waiver programs and special assistance programs that may help pay the costs. (For more on nursing home coverage, see Nolo's article on when Medicaid pays for nursing homes in North Carolina.)

Medicaid Coverage of Assisted Living Services in North Carolina

Assisted living facilities are generally less expensive and less medically intensive than nursing homes, but are not cheap by any means. Most North Carolina residents living in assisted living facilities pay their own costs. Generally speaking, Medicaid does not cover room and board fees in assisted living facilities. However, if you have little income and few assets, you may qualify for a program that helps pay for assisted living facilities.

If you are eligible for SSI and live in an assisted living facility, you may qualify for a benefit called Special Assistance (SA) that will pay for room and board expenses, up to $1,182/month, at assisted living facilities. People with dementia who live in specialized care units can receive more money each month.

A separate program, called Special Assistance In-Home (SA/IH), provides a similar benefit for low-income people who could reside in an assisted living home but want to stay in their own homes. To apply for SA or SA/IH, contact your local county Department of Social Services office.

Medicaid Coverage of Home Health Services in North Carolina

Home health care can include skilled nursing or therapy services, home health aide services like medication management or bathing assistance, and personal care aide services like meal preparation or cleaning. If you already receive Medicaid in North Carolina for doctor's and hospital visits, the program will pay for some home health services like nursing, therapy, medical supplies, and equipment. Your doctor must prescribe home health services for you as part of a plan of care for a particular condition.

Medicaid may also pay for personal care services, but only as prescribed by your doctor according to a plan of care, and only up to 80 hours/month. To qualify for personal care services, you must show that you need assistance with your activities of daily living.

Waiver programs. If you have an ongoing need for personal care services, you should apply for assistance from one of North Carolina's Medicaid waiver programs or its PACE Program (see below). North Carolina's two waiver programs are Community Alternatives Program for Disabled Adults (CAP/DA) and Community Alternatives Program/ Choice (CAP/Choice).

To qualify for either waiver, you must be 65 or older, blind, or disabled. In addition, you must show that you meet the nursing facility level of care and that you are at risk of institutionalization within 30 days.

CAP/DA. If you qualify for CAP/DA, you can receive a wide range of services like adult day health, personal care aide, home modification and mobility aids, meal preparation and delivery, respite services, personal emergency response services, transition services, assistive technology, and case management. In CAP/DA, an agency arranges your services and oversees your plan of care for you.

CAP/Choice. If you prefer to select and train your own service providers, you can participate in CAP/Choice. CAP/Choice offers all of the services that CAP/DA offers, but you have a larger role in directing your own care. To help you, CAP/Choice also pays for people to advise you, like a personal assistant, a care advisor, and a financial manager. To find out more about the CAP/DA and CAP/Choice programs, contact the "CAP/DA CAP/Choice Lead Agency" in your area.

Developmental disabilities. North Carolina has other waiver programs for individuals with developmental disabilities and for children with fragile medical conditions. For more information about these waivers, contact the Department of Health and Human Services Customer Service Center at 800-662-7030 FREE.

North Carolina's PACE Programs

Programs of All-Inclusive Care for the Elderly (PACE) currently operate in several communities in North Carolina. To qualify for PACE, you must be 55 or older, live in an area served by a PACE agency, and meet North Carolina's nursing home level of care standard, and you must be able to live safely in the community with PACE services. If you do not receive Medicaid, you can use Medicare to pay for PACE, or you can pay for the program yourself.

PACE participants receive their services from an interdisciplinary team of professionals like physicians, nurses, and social workers, whose role is to coordinate individualized care and services to keep seniors in their own homes and communities. If you receive Medicaid and participate in a PACE, Medicaid pays for all of the services recommended by your care team. If you are interested in a PACE program, contact it directly to apply. You can find a PACE program in your community here.

Wanting to Move Out of a Nursing Home?

North Carolina operates a program called the Money Follows the Person (MFP) that helps people move out of institutions and into less restrictive settings. If you are elderly or disabled, have lived in an institution for at least 90 days, and meet the nursing facility level of care, but want to live in your home or in a community-based setting, then you might qualify for assistance from the MFP program.

MFP provides a variety of services designed to help a recipient live independently in his or her home, including homemaker and chore help, day services, home accessibility adaptations, and home health aide services. To apply, call the North Carolina Money Follows the Person Project at 855-761-9030 FREE.

Supportive Services for North Carolinians Who Do Not Qualify For Medicaid

If you do not qualify for Medicaid and do not meet the nursing home level of care, you may still qualify for some services like transportation, meals, and in-home help. North Carolina's Area Agencies on Aging administer various programs that offer support to seniors.[12] (End of NOLO quote).

How Medicare Can Help You

The Medicare side is really a very different program. If you've had a qualifying hospital stay, you've got to be getting better, you have got to be recovering for Medicare to continue to pay. But the real advantage to a Medicare program – when you have home health – is you're going to get up to a 60-day spell of illness.

It's called an "intermittent spell of illness", and it's going to be paid 100% under your Part A Medicare. You might get nursing services, a physical therapist or occupational therapist, speech language pathologist, or a home health aid that comes and assists with bathing. And that's going to last for 60 days. On occasion they can be recertified for an additional 60 days, but it usually caps out at that 60-day period.

When You Need Both

There are programs where Medicare and Medicaid can overlap at certain times. There are times when people have finished their Medicare service but still need additional services. That could be through Medicaid, private pay, or long term care insurance. Clearly there is not the stringent qualification requirements for Medicare as there are for Medicaid. Whereas Medicare is available for all seniors to assist in paying for regular Doctor's visits, and emergency room and emergency procedures, and 100% of home health, with 'Assisted Living' and long term care Medicaid for seniors, there are many more costs and barriers to qualify for this benefits program.

These types of Medicaid benefits are means tested. The programs require that your income and asset levels among other qualifications meet their stringent guidelines. Also the long term care Medicaid program has a look back period of up to 5 years as of 2016, which require any cash or asset transfer within that look back period dating back from the day of application be found proper under the strict guidelines of this program. An elder law attorney can help you with qualification and give much needed advice and guidance as to how assets may be characterized to allow you to qualify for this benefit for long term care Medicaid.

The Importance of Planning Ahead

One of the most heartbreaking calls that I get is from the people that fall in that gap. They're over-resourced for Medicaid, and they're under-resourced to pay privately. Perhaps their income level doesn't allow them to roll over and let Medicaid pay for it. It's a hard place.

That's why it's important to plan ahead and make sure you're prepared, whether it's an emergency situation or simply old age. When I relate Medicaid to seniors, I'm talking about special assistance Medicaid or long-term care Medicaid, paying for nursing homes, assisted living, or in-home care. Medicare will not pay for these types of long-term care.

Medicare pays for 20 days, and that's it. And then who pays? You do. If you've got a Medicare supplement through private insurance, the supplement would pick up and pay for 80 days. So that's 100 days total that are covered. After that, you pay out of pocket. That's a scary situation,because if you have to stay there, then you have to start paying. And the cost can be tremendous.

So what is a Medicaid Crisis?

I cannot stress this statistic enough: According to a Department of Health and Human Services report, as of 2005, there's a 70% chance that people over 65 will need some type of long-term care during their lifetime. That's the reality. That means that you're going to tap your savings, your retirement savings, and have to start spending that down out of pocket.

Let's go over a scenario that qualifies as a Medicaid crisis (and please note, this is completely fictional; any resemblance to actual scenarios on the part of the readers is purely coincidental):

Imagine for a moment your Aunt Beth has a bad fall in her house. Since then, she has slowly lost her ability to walk and perform basic activities within the house, such as bathing and moving from room to room. You have been looking after your Aunt Beth since the fall occurred and she has since designated you as the power of attorney. The doctors have informed you that due to her old age, and the fact that her injuries are not getting better, she will likely need to move to a nursing home. Medicare is only going to cover the costs for the first few weeks of her stay, after which it is up to her to pay. You have absolutely no idea how much the total cost will be once Medicare stops paying, and you want to help your Aunt apply for Medicaid but you're not sure when and how to go about the process.

This is where the Medicaid crisis planning component comes in. People come to me all the time in emergency situations such as the fictional one above. They're asking me what to do, because their wife or husband has to go to a nursing home or assisted living facility and they haven't planned for it. They're being asked to spend down most of their retirement savings to qualify for Medicaid.

That's money they're expected to live on for the next 20 or 30 years. Then a lien is placed on their house and taken to satisfy their medical bills after that family member passes.

Why is Paying Out of Pocket a Big Deal?

Home healthcare agents charge on average, $21 an hour across the nation. Assisted living facilities cost about $40,000 a year across the nation, and the national average for nursing home facilities is around $76,000 on average. That's a lot of money per year. And you could have other costs and incidental costs above that. So if you're coming out of pocket $75'000 to $100,000 a year to pay for care, that could sap an estate and retirement savings fast.

When Will Medicaid Pay?

When will they come in and start helping you pay for nursing home or assisted living care? After you've spent most of your money? Let me tell you about those situations. For a nursing home or assisted living resident, you can keep $2,000 in assets. That's your resource money. That's it. You could keep your home at that time, if you tell them you intend to remain in the home or go back to the home, but that doesn't mean it won't be sold in probate to pay the Medicaid lien in the end. That's usually how it works. That's what we want to avoid. That gives the family options.

What if you're married? If there's a healthy spouse, and one spouse has to go to a nursing home or assisted living facility, the healthy spouse can keep – as of 2016 – $119,220. That's it. Now, some of you might say, well, that's a lot of money. If I poured it out on a table, it would look like a lot of money. But if you've got a good long time to live, that's not going to get you very far and provide a lifestyle you want.

A lot of people are concerned that this is way too low. You ought to be able to keep more, because you worked for it. You paid into this system. But what about the rest of the money? If you have, let's say $300,000, and you know that you can keep, as the healthy spouse, about $120,000. But your wife or husband is going to a nursing home or assisted living facility, how do you keep the rest?

The other $180,000 that you and your spouse worked so hard for, Medicaid would say, just go spend it down on healthcare, funeral costs, burial plot, headstone, or on your car. You could spend it making your house more handicap accessible. Put in a ramp, maybe bars in the bathroom, or roll-in showers.

You can prepay utility bills, or hair appointments for a year. My mom did that for my grandmother. If you have a special needs family member, you could give 100% of that money to a trust for that family member, and save 100% of the cash assets. That's another way to do it. But there are more attractive options than giving up control of that money.

What about keeping it so you could have the life and retirement you saved for all those years? Well, we can use legal and financial tools so you can have them. In the married couple situation, with a healthy spouse, we can help keep almost 100% of the cash assets.

The reason I say "almost 100%", is because with IRAs and 401ks, there could be tax consequences, but those are generally offset, for the most part, by the healthcare expenses that year. In a single person situation, where there's no spouse, we can keep 50 to 60% of the cash assets. Medicaid will come in and pay for long-term care for you. We work with families all the time to make that happen. We also want to look at saving real estate by passing it outside of the probate estate, directly to your loved ones. The last of your money stays under your control during your life and then also passes to your loved ones.

This is however, only in emergency situations, where you're in a nursing home now – or headed there quickly. And the family comes to me and says, "What are we going to do? We can't afford this healthcare for very long. How can we position ourselves so the money goes the farthest and mom gets the best care?"

That's the situation I'm talking about. If you just go to social services, they're going to tell you to spend all your money. They are just going to tell you what the law is. We work with those social workers all the time, and they're experts in what they do,but they're not attorneys. They can't give you legal advice.

You want to avoid getting in that situation where you just go to social services, and you're told you have to spend everything, and then it's gone.

Life Estate Deeds

I have made it one of my personal missions to make sure seniors who come to me are guaranteed that their assets are protected. Through the years, this has become a fundamental driving force for my practice, and I want them to reap all the benefits that are not only available to them, but are rightfully owed them.

Let's start by defining some terms, and then we can talk about why they're important to you and your estate plan.

Standard Life Estate Deeds

Under the guidelines of these deeds, you would be able to select someone close to you - a family member, for instance - as the beneficiary of your property. You, the "life tenant" would thereby grant an automatic transfer of your property to the person you elect to be the beneficiary, or the "remainderman." This person would thus be eligible to inherit your property, such as your house or whatever other asset you name, but you would retain ownership of the property as long as you were living. Standard Life Estate Deeds, however, are somewhat restrictive, in that you would have little say in what happens to that property. Say, for instance, you decide the property should be your house. You name a beneficiary for the house and it remains yours during your living days. You cannot, however, sell the house or mortgage it under the Life Estate Deed.

Also, life estate deeds do count as a countable transfer of assets that would trigger a penalty or prevent you from drawing Medicaid. If the transfer was within a look-back period, you would need to void that transfer by transferring the property back to yourself to be able to qualify for Medicaid. Even though you may now qualify for a Medicaid benefit to assist in paying for long-term care, a Medicaid lien may still be placed on your property after you pass away during the probate process. This Medicaid lien applied in probate needs to be paid and may result in the sale or auction of your property to pay the lien. Essentially, the property may not pass to your heirs but may be sold to satisfy the Medicaid lien.

Enhanced Life Estate Deeds, a.k.a. Lady Bird Deeds

What are Lady Bird Deeds? What do they do, and how do they differ from traditional deeds, like regular General Warranty Deeds or Life Estates Deeds? How do they fit into your estate planning, especially when considering the possible long-term care Medicaid scenario?

I love these deeds because they can accomplish asset protection simply, quickly and cleanly. Why are they called Lady Bird Deeds? Well, there are a couple of stories surrounding how those deeds came to be named. Of course, they are named after Lady Bird Johnson, the wife of President Lyndon B. Johnson, the commander-in-chief, originally responsible for implementing Medicaid. One rumor has it that President Johnson created this type of deed to ensure that all his property would transfer smoothly to his wife upon his death. Another story goes that the lawyer who first drafted this deed, Gerry Beyer from Florida, used the Johnson couple's names as examples when describing it, and the name just stuck. Regardless of how the name came to be, I am so thankful that they are in existence today. I will be talking about Ladybird Deeds as they exist in the legal system of North Carolina because that's the state where I practice law. However, many states in the U. S. also accept Lady Bird Deeds in much the same way. (Please refer to the list below to see if your state also accepts Lady Bird Deeds).

Medicaid can put a lien on your house and may take it when you pass if you have to draw on the system at any point to pay for long-term care. We've discussed how 70% of individuals over 65 years of age might require some kind of long-term care, whether it's in-home, assisted living care or at a nursing facility. To qualify for Medicaid, you have to spend out of your own assets or have long-term care insurance in place, and a plan to protect your assets. Lady Bird Deeds can help steer you clear of losing your home at your passing to pay off the lien Medicaid would put on that house.

Let's compare Lady Bird Deeds to some of the other deeds. There are General Warranty Deeds or Regular Fee Simple Deeds, which is when you pass everything to a grantee or whomever you appoint. A Lady Bird Deed is the best of both worlds. They allow you to reserve a life interest in a property but qualifies or defines that life interest like a fee simple full-ownership interest. You can still mortgage, sell, or gift the property and even unilaterally extinguish the future interest holder. You can control it fully, you can sell the property away out from under the future interest holders which might be, for instance, your children without them signing off on the sale. That is different from any other deed I have seen drafted. It's a totally different concept. It's withholding the power to convey the property, 100% of the proceeds, without the grantee, the interest holder signing off. It extinguishes their interest. For instance, with a Traditional Life Estate Deed, you cannot even lay waste to the property, that means if it's got timber on it, you can't clear it off. You have to keep the house in good repair because the future interest holder has an interest in that property. With a Lady Bird Deed you do not. You can lay waste to the property, you can do whatever you want. You can sell it, mortgage it, and the future interest holder can't say anything about it. It's a great deal for the senior and automatic protection from the look back period for Medicaid benefit qualification purposes.

As mentioned above, a Medicaid lien can attach to your property when it passes through the probate and estate administration process. However, because you are passing the property outside of the probate and administration process, no lien may attach (check to see if your state is an expanded recovery state allowing the acquisition of property passed outside of probate to satisfy outstanding liens). Because you, the Grantor, retain the full ability to sell the property and keep the proceeds or mortgage the property without the Grantee(s), beneficiary or beneficiaries signing off on the transfer, you have not therefore, given away their power to appoint the property. When you give away your power of appointment, it's a countable asset transfer under the long term Medicaid look back period. Alongside a kind and generous policy of the retirement friendly states that allow them, the Lady Bird Deed is not a countable asset transfer under the Medicaid rules.

Lady Bird Deeds work very well in North Carolina right now, and are a reliable and allowable planning tool in other states. In addition to North Carolina, the following are states that recognize Lady Bird Deeds[13]:

▶ Arizona

▶ Arkansas

▶ California

▶ Colorado

▶ Florida

▶ Hawaii

▶ Kansas

▶ Minnesota

▶ Missouri

▶ Montana

▶ Nevada

▶ New Mexico

▶ North Carolina

▶ Ohio

▶ Oklahoma

▶ Texas

▶ Wisconsin

[13]http://www.lawlesher.com/lady-bird-deed/

States such as Georgia, however, frown upon Lady Bird Deeds. They don't allow them. At this point in time, they are legal in North Carolina and it's a very, very good way, especially in an emergency situation, to transfer assets. There is a possibility in the future that the law will change, but that's always a possibility.

There are other more advanced ways to shield property, such as Medicaid asset protection trusts (MAPT). This is a simple way to transfer property and still qualify for Medicaid, while not allowing the Medicaid lien to apply against your property. So what should you do? Some people work for 30 years to pay off their home. Most people put a lot of work into their property. By doing nothing, you risk losing your home you've worked for.

If this risk were to materialize and come to pass, you would essentially be losing the American Dream. Your home is part of that dream. Protect it by getting your property deeds in proper order. You can do that by using Life Estate Deeds, Lady Bird Deeds and other strategies, which can help save your property, but only if you take action.

A Medicaid benefit look back period, which is 5 years for nursing home Medicaid in North Carolina, is important in pre-planning to protect your hard earned money and property. All countable asset transfers under the Medicaid rules must be made outside this look back period so planning ahead is key. Lady Bird Deeds can offer relief from a look back period while they are allowable. The clock is ticking, so it's in your best interest to contact an elder law attorney before more precious time slips out of your hands.

Using Medicaid Compliant Annuities to Save Your Money from a Medicaid Spend-Down

I have mentioned repeatedly that I am in the business of protecting your assets and ensuring you and your family have the planning tools to save you from the headache awaiting if you're not prepared in the event of a healthcare incident. For this chapter, I would like to enlist the help of my friends at Krause Financial Services. They feature a fantastic explanation on their website of another tool I want to bring to your attention: a Medicaid Compliant Annuity.

As many of you know, annuities can be a great relief to families because they turn your extra resources or spend-down amount into an income stream. Although this is an option not offered by every insurance company, I highly suggest you look into what your insurance company's policies are regarding this important tool and the Medicaid laws in your state. So let's get into the definition and the eligibility surrounding a Medicaid Complaint Annuity.

In its simplest terms, a Medicaid Compliant annuity eliminates the need for a person to spend-down assets to qualify for Medicaid. We sometimes see this scenario with married couples where one is healthier than the other. Say, for instance, you have a husband and wife, and the wife is much healthier than her husband. Because of her good health, she is not considering retirement, and continues to work and generate an income. Her husband, on the other hand, no longer works due to his health. Think back to the means-tested approach to Medicaid, due to the wife's income, the husband might not have qualified for the coverage he needs. The test would have stated that he is of sufficient means to pay for the assistance; and therefore would not receive the annuity that could be used toward the price of his healthcare assistance.

Medicaid Compliant annuities provide for the complete opposite. The wife could continue to receive an income, and her husband would receive the Medicaid annuity he needs to help pay for the long-term care assistance. The wife's income would therefore have no bearing on whether her husband qualifies for Medicaid. How is this possible, you ask? Let's turn to Krause Financial Services to help with the explanation.

According to Krause, once the spend-down amount is eliminated by converting it into an income stream, "the nursing home resident/Medicaid applicant becomes eligible for Medicaid benefits". The annuity is therefore a "single premium immediate annuity with an added restrictions endorsement", which makes the annuity "irrevocable and non-assignable"[14]. The language associated with this tool came to be in 1994 with the drafting of Transmittal 64 by the Secretary of Health Care Financing Administration. In the document, the following was stated:

Annuities, although usually purchased in order to provide a source of income for retirement, are occasionally used to shelter assets so that individuals purchasing them can become eligible for Medicaid. In order to avoid penalizing annuities validly purchased as part of a retirement plan but to capture those annuities which abusively shelter assets, a determination must be made with regard to the ultimate purpose of the annuity (i.e., whether the purchase of the annuity constitutes a transfer of assets for less than fair market value). If the expected return on the annuity is commensurate with a reasonable estimate of the life expectancy of the beneficiary, the annuity can be deemed actuarially sound.[15]

What does it mean for an annuity to be "actuarially sound"? It means the annuity cannot exceed the Medicaid life expectancy of the owner, or person receiving the annuity. Most states look upon this rule as favorable, except for four: North Dakota, Oregon,

[14]https://www.medicaidannuity.com/products/medicaid-compliant-annuity/
[15]Healthcare Financing Administration, State Medicaid Manual 3257-3259 "Transmittal 64"

Washington, and Illinois, with Illinois being the most recent state to propose moving away from these terms.

Yet another provision of the Medicaid Compliant annuity has to do with the passing of the remainder of that annuity amount, which could be to the person's child or spouse depending on the situation. It is required that the owner of the annuity name the state as the primary beneficiary of the annuity, but the secondary beneficiary may be someone of the owner's choosing, perhaps their child. Remember, the annuity will pay through the penalty period before Medicaid will come in and provide benefits. Therefore, the state is owed nothing as the beneficiary and receives nothing because they have not paid any benefits before the death of the annuity owner. The secondary beneficiary which could be a family member, receives the balance of the annuity not yet paid. Again, these are very specific circumstances, so let's now get into the differences that arise between single people and married couples when it comes to Medicaid Compliant Annuities.

Single Person

If the owner of the annuity is single and does not have any children, the state must still be named the primary beneficiary of the annuity. This is how the scenario plays out: say the owner of the annuity, a single person with no children, dies before he or she has received all the money provisioned under that annuity. The state, being the primary beneficiary, would receive no monies because they have yet to begin paying benefits and are owed nothing. The secondary beneficiary, (whoever named), would receive the remaining monies left in the annuity.

Through the Medicaid Compliant annuity, you can ensure that, as a rule of thumb, between one half and 60% of the total liquid assets over $2,000 are converted into an income stream, while the other half can be gifted to a family member or several family members.

Just because you are not married and have no children doesn't mean there is no one you care about and want to provide for after you pass away.

Married Couple

As stated briefly above, the Medicaid Compliant annuity helps couples in which one spouse continued to receive an income, while the other was unable to and incurred healthcare costs. In contrast to the options available to a single person, a married individual can absolutely, and *should*, name his or her spouse the payee and beneficiary of the annuity or annuities. I encourage you to find out what your insurance company offers and the provisions enacted in your state.

So how exactly is it determined how much the spouses can keep? Let's again use the example of the senior married couple, where the wife continues to work but the husband is not able to. Say the husband, we'll call him Mr. Johnson in honor of the Lady Bird Deeds I love so much, has to enter a nursing home. In order to qualify for those Medicaid benefits, Mr. Johnson cannot have more than $2,000 in assets (this maximum amount might differ from state to state). The wife - who would be referred to as the "community spouse" in this situation, can also keep assets, but can only keep one-half of them. Everything that is quantifiable, the wife retains half of that figure, with the maximum retention number being just over $119,220 in North Carolina.

Overall, it can be possible to save close to 100% of the total assets of the married couple for the use and benefit of the community/ healthy spouse for his/her use and benefit.

Types of Medicaid Compliant Annuity Payouts

In closing, I will call upon my friends at Krause Financial Services once again to help me explain the types of payouts provided by the Medicaid Compliant Annuities. Here are your three options:

Life-Only Payout: This type of payout ensures that the owner will receive the annuity payments for as long as he or she is still alive. Once the owner passes away, the payments stop.

Period Certain Payout: As part of this type of payout, the owner agrees upon a specified period of time in which he or she will receive the installments. Once that period of time expires, the owner ceases to receive any payments. Should the owner die before the period certain payout time elapses, the named beneficiary would continue to receive those installments for the rest of that period.

Life and Period Certain Payout: Just as it sounds, this is a combination of the two types listed above. The owner first establishes a period of time in which he or she will receive the installments, let's say 5 years. If the owner lives past the 5 years, then he or she can still claim the installments for as long as he or she is living. The terms also still stand if the owner were to pass away before the 5-year period; a named beneficiary would receive those payments until the 5 years were up.

In summation, I urge you to speak to your elder law attorney no matter if you are single or married to find out if a Medicaid Compliant Annuity is right for you. You want to do as much as you can to avoid the headache and the additional incurred costs that unfortunately befall so many people during a Medicaid crisis. Use the tools that were outlined in this chapter to really stock your arsenal and protect all of your hard-earned money and assets.

CHAPTER 7

Veterans Benefits

I have something very special for you in this chapter, something very near and dear to my heart. You may know that I'm a veteran myself and spent four years in the Navy. Absolutely loved it. My dad was in the Navy, stationed in San Diego, just as I was. My grandfather (**J. C. Horne, my mother's father**) was in World War II, and I have an interview with him to share with you. Before we get to the interview, I would like to address the benefits currently available to our veterans.

Aid and Attendance: What Benefits Are Available for Veterans

VA Aid and Attendance is a program where a veteran, the spouse of a veteran, or spouse of a deceased veteran who has to have day-to-day care, can get a monthly monetary benefit paid to them. The term is pretty self-explanatory, as it applies to individuals who need the aid and the attendance of another person to help them with their daily activities. Aid and Attendance is a monthly payment paid in addition to an individual's pension, so it goes without saying that to receive the Aid and Attendance the person must first be receiving a pension. So to qualify, one must meet certain qualifications. A doctor can be involved in the qualification decision. However, if the veteran is in an assisted living facility or nursing home, they automatically meet the initial qualifications but will need to meet other criteria as well.

There are three tiers of additional aid that are offered to veterans and the people that meet the requirements. In this section, I will call on a few organizations to help define the Aid and Attendance tier. The remaining two tiers will be explained later in the chapter.

According to the U.S. Department of Veterans Affairs, at least one of the following is needed for an individual to qualify to begin receiving the additional payment of Aid and Attendance:

▶ The individual must prove that he/she requires the aid and attendance of someone else to carry out basic daily functions such as bathing and getting dressed.
▶ The individual must be disabled to the point of being bedridden.
▶ The individual must be admitted to a nursing home due to the inability to provide basic care for himself/herself.
▶ The individual must record an eyesight of 5/200 or below in both eyes. Individual must therefore be significantly visually impaired.
▶ Again, the individual can qualify for Aid and Attendance if he/she meets one of the following conditions listed above.[16]

Of course, the maximum amount that individuals will receive once qualified for Aid and Attendance differs on a case by case basis. Below is a table of the current maximum monthly benefit amount:

[16]http://www.benefits.va.gov/pension/aid_attendance_housebound.asp

BENEFIT TABLE

STATUS	MONTHLY BENEFIT AMOUNT
Surviving Spouse	$1,149
Single Veteran	$1,788
Married Veteran	$2,120
Two Vets Married	$2,837

Benefits accurate as of the date of drafting unless otherwise indicated and updated.

The asset level threshold is another requirement needed to qualify for Aid and Attendance assistance. The rule of thumb of the threshold is generally accepted as being below $80,000, but we believe it's really around $20,000. However, there are ways under the rules to position assets and still qualify for Aid and Attendance assistance.

You can make smart decisions to hold on to your hard earned money and property while still enjoying the benefits of the extra income.

If you're a veteran, and have served ninety (90) days of active duty, one (1) day beginning or ending during a period of War, you may be eligible for the Aid and Attendance benefit.

Here is a link to all war time events that the Veterans Administration has designated for A&A benefits: http://www.veteranaid.org/docs/Periods_of_War.pdf

I would qualify because I was in the military during the window for the Gulf War. That qualifies me for Aid and Attendance if I ever needed the benefit. It also qualifies my spouse, andeven if I passed away, she'd still be eligible for that benefit through me.

Of course, that's just me. You should check the resources to see if you qualify for this very beneficial program. Eligibility must be proven by filing the proper Veterans Application for Pension or Compensation. This application will require a copy of DD-214 or separation papers, Medical Evaluation from a physician, current medical issues, net worth limitations and net income, along with out-of-pocket Medical Expenses.

In order to qualify financially, an applicant must have on average less than $80,000 in assets, excluding their home and vehicles.

Checklist for Veterans Aid & Attendance Benefits:

Veteran? Spouse of Veteran? Spouse of deceased veteran?

_____

_____

_____

At least 90 days of active duty service?

_____

_____

_____

At least one day of active duty service during a wartime event. Service does not have to be in a combat theater?

_____

_____

_____

Under $20,000 in assets, excluding home. Consult an Elder Law Attorney for strategic legal planning and advice?

_____

_____

_____

A current need: At least 2 out of 6 standard ADLs impaired:

ADLs:

- ▶ **Eating?**
- ▶ **Preparing Meals?**
- ▶ **Walking?**
- ▶ **Dressing?**
- ▶ **Bathing?**
- ▶ **Toileting?**

A physician must sign an FL2 form confirming current need.

_____

_____

_____

Proposed Changes to the VA Pension Eligibility Rules

I am an extremely proud American. I have served my country and continue to do well by my fellow citizens by providing information and services to guarantee preparedness in the event of a healthcare crisis. For this reason, I believe it is a basic American right to know when legislation is introduced that affects a large group of people. That group should know the ins and outs of what is written and how it can affect them.

In this case, I'm speaking specifically about the proposed changes to the VA Pension Eligibility, changes that were put on the table on January 23, 2015, by the Department of Veteran Affairs. As many of you may know, the VA Pension Eligibility is a needs-based program, and the benefits awarded to the veterans and their families have provided a huge amount of help to these individuals throughout the years. We would want to take care of our elderly veterans who risked their lives to ensure we sleep soundly at night. So allow me this opportunity to go through these proposed changes and explain how it impacts you if you're a veteran or the family member of a veteran.

Current Reading of the Law

Since 1980, the law has read that to qualify for the benefits, a veteran needs to have served a minimum of 24 months, and at least one of those days would have to be actively served during a "wartime period". Veterans who have been dishonorably discharged do not qualify.[17]

Allowances can be made for veterans 65 years of age and older, who have a permanent disability. In terms of income, the veteran's household income cannot exceed the amount the veteran is trying to qualify for in assistance and benefits. Much of the language regarding income has to do with countable income. If you are not sure how to calculate the figure, refer to the table later in this chapter for an example of how to find this figure.

---

[17]www.federalregister.gov

So now we know the current legislation, let us get to the proposed changes.

What Might Change

Below are some proposed changes that have been rumored for Veterans Aid and Attendance benefits qualifications. These changes, if imposed, would make it harder for a veteran to qualify and allow the veteran to keep and protect less money and property. Examine the list of proposed changes below:

A clear net worth limit. The VA proposed that the net worth limit a veteran can claim when applying for the Eligibility program cannot exceed $119,220. This is actually the same amount that a community spouse is allowed to have when applying for Medicaid.

Income and net worth calculation. The Federal Register has very graciously provided an example breakdown of how calculations will be made. First off, the VA will calculate income to establish the pension entitlement, and will "subtract all applicable deductible expenses to include appropriate prospective medical expenses". When calculating the net worth, the VA will take the annual income and add it to the assets. For instance, let's say a veterans net worth limit is $115,000. The annual income of the spouse is $7,000 and the total assets are $116,000. The total net worth would come to $123,000, which exceeds the net worth limit by $8,000.[18]

Exempt asset. A primary residence will not be included as an asset in the calculation of net worth, as long as the residence sits on an area that does not exceed 2 acres. Right now there is now limit on the acreage of the primary residence and it is exempt from the net worth calculation.

If you would like to read the full legislation, go to FederalRegister. gov and read their article entitled "Net Worth, Asset Transfers, and Income Exclusions for Needs-Based Benefits". I strongly urge you, if you are a veteran or you are the spouse or child of one, to sift through the newly proposed changes to see how you might be impacted.

Surviving Spouses

Another question that I often get concerns the surviving spouses of veterans. What happens if the veteran in the family is of good health, yet the spouse is having healthcare problems and incurs staggering medical bills? Luckily, there is support available for the spouses. According to veteranaid.org, the spouse of a veteran who incurs healthcare costs is eligible to receive no more than $1,149 each month. Similarly, a veteran that has a sick spouse is eligible to receive no more than $1,406 each month. Please note that these are the figures which were made available as of January 1, 2015.[19]

Veterans Improved Pension: Other Tiers

As mentioned, there are two other tiers within the Veterans Improved Pension program. The first is known as the Basic Pension, which extends to veterans over the age of 65 who are disabled. The Basic Pension also extends to the surviving spouse of the veteran as long as he/she meets the income qualifications. The following are the countable income requirements that the veteran must meet. Please note that these are the figures given by VeteranAid.org as of January 1, 2015.

▶ A single veteran's countable income cannot exceed $12,465 annually.

▶ A married veteran's countable income cannot exceed $16,324 annually.

The second tier is known as the Housebound Pension. Just like the other tiers, there are qualifications that must be met to be eligible to receive the monthly amount. Housebound Pension recipients must prove they require assistance of another individual in their home, (they do this by having their primary physician sign off that they need the aid), but they are not as limited in their day to day actions as those that receive the Aid and Assistance Pension.

The following are the conditions that must be met regarding the countable income of the veteran:

▶ A single veteran's countable income must not exceed $15,233 annually.
▶ A married veteran's countable income must not exceed $19,093 annually.

When speaking about countable income, it is imperative that you record all your expenses. The VA discourages individuals from paying various expenses in cash, that way you maintain a paper trail and can add this to your countable income. One issue I have found is there are individuals who are not clear on how to properly calculate their countable income. Please refer to the next section if you are curious on how to calculate this figure.

Calculating your Countable Income

Thanks to VeteranAid.org, there is a comprehensive chart you can download from their website and print out if you want to do the arithmetic the classic way, with pen and paper. I have reproduced the information below for your convenience.

The first step is to estimate the total annual income of the veteran, whether single or married. When figuring this total, you are to consider the following:

What to include in the calculation
▶ All income including social security, pension, interest income, dividends, income from rental properties, etc.
▶ CDs, annuities, stocks, bonds, savings/checking, IRAs, etc.
▶ Assets owned by the spouse

What NOT to include in the calculation:

▶ Residence or vehicle when calculating the net worth

▶ Life insurance policy

When all the above is taken into consideration, you get the estimated annual income of the veteran.

The second step is to add up all the recurring healthcare expenses incurred by the veteran each month. This includes the following:

▶ Assisted Living costs

▶ Nursing home costs

▶ Home Care service costs

▶ Health Insurance premium

▶ Medicare premium

▶ Monthly prescription costs

The individual then adds up these monthly costs and multiplies by 12 to get the annual healthcare expenses.

The third step is to subtract the annual healthcare expenses from the annual income. The equation looks like this:

Total annual income - Total annual healthcare expenses = countable income

This amount is used to determine the veteran's eligibility for one of the three tiers of the Pension program.[20]

[20]http://www.veteranaid.org/docs/income.pdf

Spotlight on: Veterans and the American Legion

I had the wonderful pleasure of sitting down with Evan Thompson, the District Commander for the American Legion of Cleveland and Rutherford Counties. Evan took the time out of his schedule to discuss with me the needs of our veterans in the community. We also touched on how you can get involved in the American Legion and how groups such as his are serving veterans in their respective communities.

Evan has a rich background stemming from his time spent in the Marine Corps. When he came out of the Marine Corps, he joined the North Carolina Air National Guard, which he would later claim was not a smart move for him. After realizing this, Evan went to the Marine Reserves where he spent one year before moving on to the Army Reserves in 1976.

What were your duties as part of the Army Reserves?

I was an infantry training instructor, so I taught things like mechanized infantry, 50-caliber machine guns, and things like that. I stayed in the Army Reserve until 1992, and during that time I went back on active duty with the Army and I spent one extended tour at Fort Jackson training soldiers for an entire training cycle. I also did a tour of duty at Anniston, Alabama, at the Chemical and Biological Warfare Center. I therefore had a very long career, 23 years. I retired in 1992 as a Brigade Sergeant Major with the rank of Command Sergeant Major. I enjoyed it all, and I loved my military service. I think military service gives people skills that they wouldn't otherwise have.

Now you're in the American Legion, working as the District Commander. Let's talk about some of the great things the American Legion does.

The American Legion is such a great organization, and I have only one regret about it: that I didn't join earlier than I actually did. I've only been a member 5 years and had I known what the American Legion does, how beneficial it is to veterans, I would have joined a long time ago. So I think one of the best things a veteran can do today is join the American Legion.

There are obviously a number of veteran service organization, such as the Marine Corps League, the VFW, DAV, all those are great organizations; but the American Legion is the largest veteran service organization boasting a membership of over 2.4 million not only in the United States but in foreign countries, as well. The American Legion is also based on four pillars, which really determine what the Legion does. They are: Americanism, national security, children and youth, and veterans and veterans' benefits. To give you an idea of what's in those pillars, for instance, one of the main programs from the Americanism pillar is our baseball program, and we're fortunate in Shelby, NC, to be the home of the American Legion World Series. That is a tremendous honor and it's something that not too many services can boast. The Series brings so much to the economy of Cleveland County during that time of year, and the support from the community and volunteers is incredible.

What are some other benefits offered by the American Legion?

Of course, things we like to really focus on in the American Legion is helping our veterans and helping our youth. These can be children or grandchildren of veterans, but it's not limited to that. That's one thing about the American Legion: you don't have to be a member to get the benefits that the Legion has to provide. One thing I want to point out to everyone regarding the GI Bill; the American Legion is responsible for bringing that piece of legislation about. That's been a very important piece of legislation in many veterans' lives. I know for me, when I got out of the service, I already had my Bachelor's, but I got my Master's degree, then worked on my 6-year Specialist degree, then I had some time left and went back to get an Associate's, followed by some work on my Doctorate. The GI Bill paid for most of that, which is a tremendous benefit.

The Legion is also responsible for the development of the legislation that brought about the VA Healthcare system, and so lots of veterans enjoy benefits from that. So if you are a veteran and not tried to enter the VA Healthcare system, you need to make an application to that.

Many veterans who are just coming out of their service don't know about this system and what is available to them. It could be because they don't have major healthcare issues at the time. But one thing about eligibility is you have to have served over 180 days of active duty to be eligible, and then the healthcare system has categories. There are 8 categories, and based on your physical condition, whether or not you served in combat, whether you have a service-connected disability, and others all determine the category that you're placed into. From there, if you're in category 8 like I am - I don't have any disabilities connected to my service - you'd thus have to pay co-pays as a result, which are very small. Pretty soon, I'm going to be able to get hearing aids, which I need badly and the VA is going to pay for all of that. That's a tremendous savings for me, all because I was a veteran.

How does one get into the American Legion?

To be qualified for the American Legion, you have to have at least one day of service during a war time period. Now, there are very few periods that were not war time periods since 1917. One period in there is between 1955 and 1960, we were not engaged in conflicts anywhere. So those are the veterans that kind of fall through the cracks when it comes to being a member of the American Legion, but this is just the way that Congress chartered the American Legion. There's nothing we can do about it; we'd love to have you as a member, but according to the charter, you're not qualified.

So if you would like to become a member of the American Legion and you qualify as such, there are several things you can do.

Many times, you'll get information as a veteran from the American Legion and you can sign up, but when you do that, you're not assigned to your local post. You're assigned to a pool of American Legion members down in Raleigh. What I can do for you is if you happen to be in that situation - and there are quite a few people that are in that situation - if you'd like to transfer to Post 82, then I can do that for you. You just need to give me a call at (704) 484-2902. If you want to become a member, you can call that same number. The reason we use that number is we don't have anyone down at the post during the day; we meet once a month on the second Monday of each month, so there's no one there at the post most of the time. We therefore give out my phone number for people to call, and I'd certainly love to have you as a member of the American Legion. This is what we're here for: we're here to serve vets, and if you become a member, then you'll be serving other vets.

What are some of the other programs available?

One of the incredible programs we have under the youth pillar is called Boys' State, which is a great program we have down at Catawba College to train young men who want to learn more about the government of the state and the country. It's a good item to have on your application for college, too, especially if the young men are applying to a military academy. You're given ten additional points for entry if you've completed Boys' State.

Another thing we carry on is the Oratorical Contest every year. Students from all the local high schools can get involved in this contest, and if they win and go all the way up to the national competition, they can win up to an $18,000 scholarship. Students can get their speeches ready and participate in this exceptional program.

I can only encourage people to become a part of the American Legion because it's an organization that I'm totally dedicated to, and I'm willing at any point in time to help any veteran in any way that I can. As District Commander, I have 8 posts under my jurisdiction, and those are posts all the way from Chimney Rock down to King's Mountain. I'm not the commander of those posts, but I help the post in every way that I can. I've become the liaison between the State Department American Legion and the local posts.

Our meetings are once a month, the second Monday night of each month. So if you can't contact me, feel free to come to our post. It's at 1628 South Lafayette Street in Shelby. We'd love to have you as a guest! We always have a meal before our meetings, too. Our Christmas party is coming up, so it's going to be a little different for this year's party. We're growing, and we're about to outgrow it, which is why we're having this year's party over at the VFW.

If you'd like more information about these benefits, please contact our office at (704) 259-7040, and we can get the Veterans' Aid and Attendance information out to you, as well as American Legion information to you.

As a reminder, Veterans Aid and Attendance benefits are provided to veterans who have served at least one day of war time service. This doesn't mean they have to be in a combat zone - they could be stationed in Nebraska at an Air Force Base. But they have served at least one day during a war time event, and they meet the proper criteria: They have a healthcare situation where they may have someone caring for them at home, such as a husband or wife. Or it could also be a nursing home or assisted living situation. This can add a maximum benefit of around $2,800 to a married veteran's income. It's a great way to help care for the veterans, even adding income to the mix when a spouse is caring for the veteran. It's also available for the spouse of a veteran or the spouse of a deceased veteran.

Interview with World War II Veteran, My Grandfather, J. C. Horne:

Now that we have covered the important information, I would like to show you the interview I did with my Grandpa Papa J, who was a veteran of World War II. I was extremely close to him. He passed away when I was 13 years old. His name was J. C. Horne, and the initials stood for Jonathan Chivous, however the doctor only wrote J. C. on his birth certificate. Papa J was what I called him; everybody knew him as Jay or J. C.

I've always found if I really start concentrating on something and looking at a specific area of law, business, or anything else, everything related to that one thing seems to shift suddenly and comes into view or pops out at me.

So I started searching for this old cassette tape that I had of the interview. Once we found it, I converted it to digital, to have it for posterity.

I've e-mailed it to my family members and now I would like to share it with you. So without further ado, here's the transcription of my interview with J. C. Horne, World War II veteran.

J. C.:

It was December the 7th, 1941, on a Sunday morning. I was sitting, listening to the radio. They broke in saying Pearl Harbor had been bombed by the Japanese. I, like most people, didn't even know where Pearl Harbor was. So they finally told me where it was. Like I said, I was only 15 years old. It didn't really affect me that much. But before I knew it, I was 18 years old. I was 18 February the 24th, 1944. Two months later, I was in the service.

I Went to Ft. Bragg, was inducted and sent to Camp Blanding, Florida. It took 16 weeks of basic training. I went to Camp McCoy, Wisconsin, and on Thanksgiving Day of 1944, I boarded the ship for Europe. We didn't know where we were going. They didn't tell us until we got halfway across. So we landed in Portsmouth, England, a southern resort equivalent to our Miami, Florida. We stayed there 'til Christmas. Then we left for Le Havre, France. We went from there to the Battle of the Bulge.

So we relieved another division, then went to Luxemburg. From then on, we went into the Siegfried Line. At about March, they started letting guys, one at a time in the company, get a pass right off the front lines. You had a choice of Brussels, Paris, or London. So I took four days in Paris, and had to go right back on the front lines again. At that time, the war was winding down. Still war was going on but by that time it wasn't that severe. And we started taking a lot of prisoners everywhere we went. We knew it wouldn't be long until the war would be over then. And the war was over a little later, in April. In the meantime, they put us on displaced persons camps, guarding them and looking after them.

We did that, for about a month. Then to my disbelief, they said we were going home. We were waiting to go to the Pacific. In the meantime, they dropped an atomic bomb in the Pacific, right before we left to go to the Pacific. Our orders changed, we got to go home after they dropped the bomb.

I was very, very happy. And I got home and I was about the happiest person in the world, I guess. I knew a little later I'd be getting a discharge.

Greg:
"Could you tell us about some of your experiences during the war?"

J. C.:
I was a machine gunner, .30 caliber. The same type they used in World War I. It didn't fire as fast as the German machine gun, but it was very accurate. You could pinpoint a target by going up a click, down a click, left a click, right a click. You could just about drop something in their pocket.

Every third shell would be a tracer. That's where you could see it glow, light up, so you could see what you were hitting. It just looked like a stream of fire with every third tracer glowing like that. And that's what we did mostly. The infantry went ride ahead of us. And we sat down where we could give them covering fire and shoot over their heads. It was like we were on a hill and they were going down in the valley. They'd take towns and we'd give them covering fire.

One person would carry the tripod and one ammo. You strapped it onto your back with a board with straps on it. Two cases of ammo were on that. The other person carried the machine gun. When you had to mount the gun, we sat our parts down and we mounted them so it would be ready to fire in a matter of seconds. So that's what I did.

In the meantime, machine guns would always catch a lot of mortar fire and artillery fire. So my helmet looked like it'd been hit with a hammer all over it. We dug down and shrapnel hit your helmet, you know. Where if you hadn't ducked down, might have wiped you out. See, the blast went up like that. Then you hit the ground. If it doesn't hit right on you, you're all right. You had the 88's coming in; you could hear that, a screaming sound. And you got to where you could tell exactly where they were going. If it got to a certain level and started fading away, you were okay. If it got louder and louder and started screaming, you knew it was coming close. You hit the ground. Until it hit the ground, you stayed there. Sometimes it knocked tops of trees out and everything all around you.

Greg:

"Could you tell us about your foxholes and where you stayed during that time?"

J. C.:

Well, we had to dig the gun in every time and especially at night, we'd have one person on the gun. The squad had one on the gun all the time. And the rest of us slept. After you spent two hours on the gun, you'd go wake the next man. He'd spend two hours, he'd wake the next person up. By the time that comes around, it's your turn again. Every night, when you would be on the gun watching for something, seemed like about every tree in the distance would move. You'd think it might be somebody. You'd be watching that tree, and it seemed like it moved.

Near the end of the war, when we knew it was about over, it wasn't over, but we had met hundreds of German troops, with their commanding officer in front, walking right toward us to give up. We'd just motion them back to the rear. We didn't have time to fool with them.

Most of the time, the commander would be a general or something. They didn't want to be captured by the Russians.

Greg:

"What would the Russians have done to them?"

J. C.:

They treated them very, very mean for the simple reason, the Germans treated them that way. So they were very afraid of the Russians. They knew they'd take their anger out on them.

*** END OF INTERVIEW ***

Even today, reading through the transcript of that interview gives me chills. I loved that man with all my heart and he was my buddy. It is hard for me to believe that the gentle man I knew and loved as my grandfather experienced such atrocities. I try to imagine what a vacation of four (4) days in Paris must have been like when you had been fighting on the front lines during the War in Europe.

We owe our veterans our freedoms. Without veterans like my grandfather we may not have a great country to call home. The world would be a more dangerous and much different than it is today. It is our duty, my duty to take care of our veterans. Veterans have too few benefits. They should be able to access what benefits are available with ease. It is the least we can do for the sacrifices they made.

Many who have been in war time situations whether on the front lines or not, may be eligible for the little known benefit of Aid and Attendance, so it is best to investigate your eligibility with the Veterans Administration and an Elder Law Attorney.

CHAPTER 8

Estate Taxes: To Plan or not to Plan? There is No Question!

Estate tax is an area of finance I encourage all my clients to read up on and gain knowledge of the ins and outs of what is a very complex subject. I will do my best to break it down for you, relying on the help of data and tidbits available through the IRS as well as other federal groups.

An estate tax is a "tax on your right to transfer property at your death"[21]. Upon your death, the value of everything you own is counted and totaled, the sum of which makes up what the IRS calls your "Gross Estate." It is important to note, however, that this number comes from the most recent valuation of your items, not necessarily the price you paid for them when you made the purchase. The items that go into the total valuation in your Gross Estate include (but are not limited to) "cash and securities, real estate, insurance, trusts, annuities, and business interests."[22]

After the Gross Estate is calculated, you may then be eligible to make certain deductions from that total number. These eligible deductions include (but are not limited to) "mortgages and other

[21]http://www.irs.gov/Businesses/Small-Businesses-&-Self-Employed/Estate-Tax
[22]http://www.irs.gov/Businesses/Small-Businesses-&-Self-Employed/Estate-Tax

debts, estate administration expenses, property that passes to surviving spouses, and qualified charities."[23] Once the deductions are made, you therefore arrive at your net amount.

The way the law reads, you can now give $5.43 million dollars to an heir through your estate and incur no estate taxes whatsoever. As of 2015, this $5.43 million was set as the maximum estate tax exemption; any individual that possesses assets that total an amount over the $5.43 million will be taxed at a rate of 40%.

By now you might be asking, what is the importance of thinking about estate tax planning when deciding how to leave your hard earned assets to your children and grandchildren? There's an easy answer for that: you have to plan for it. It's negligent not to think about it and have a financial advisor and attorney help you to look at the future.

Change is constant. That's one thing we can be sure of. Even if the limit is $5.43 million dollars today, we know that policies change. Laws are repealed. It happens all the time. One regime will be exchanged for another regime in Washington and at the state level. Throughout history, laws and policies have differed with each new administration. This means we have to anticipate the potential increase or decrease of estate tax from the current $5.43 million dollars, so make sure that your attorney and financial planner or advisor thinks about those factors when you are crafting an estate plan. These two professionals should be working together: The attorney to develop the vehicle to get you where you want to go and the financial planner to fill that vehicle with gas.

Estate Tax Through History

What has the estate tax been historically? Let's look at a publication from the IRS entitled The Estate Tax: 90 Years and Counting[24], which was written by some of the experts in the field. It says, "For the past

[23]http://www.irs.gov/Businesses/Small-Businesses-&-Self-Employed/Estate-Tax
[24]http://www.irs.gov/pub/irs-soi/ninetyestate.pdf

ninety years, and at key points throughout our American history, the federal government has relied on estate and inheritance tax as a source of funding." That first line tells you something immediately. The federal government is looking at estate tax as a revenue and source of funding. As someone who has planned and worked your entire life to accumulate assets, you've got to know that the government is looking at this as an income stream. Just looking at that quote, you know the $5.43 million dollar cap will eventually decrease. If you want to predict the future, look at the past.

Getting back to the IRS publication, we see that it says, "Proponents have frequently advocated that these taxes are effective tools for preventing the concentration of wealth in the hands of relatively few powerful families, while opponents believe the transfer tax discourages capital accumulation, curbing national and economic growth. This tension, along with fiscal and other considerations, has led to periodic revisions of federal estate tax laws affecting both the size of the decedent [deceased] population subject to the tax and revenue collected."

The end of the first paragraph shows you two sides of this coin. While the sum may be $5.43 million dollars right now, when the other side comes in with the opposing view, it's going to go lower. It's going to be used to collect revenue to run the government. Again, this is straight from the IRS's website. Essentially, the taxing authority is telling you these things fluctuate. It's logical to think those in power funded by people with these views are going to vote in accordance with them and with their party.

Yet even within the United States, estate tax is not a new concept. In this paper, it points out that estate tax can be traced back to ancient Egypt, as early as 700 B.C. Nearly two thousand years ago, Roman emperor Caesar Augustus imposed the Veselina Hereditation, a tax on succession and legacies to all but close relatives.

We should have been planning for these things back two thousand years ago. It's not a new idea. You need to plan. Governments will use this as a way to fund everything from schools to wars and every other kind of initiative. One of the most interesting parts of the document is Figure C, which shows significant estate tax law changes from 1916 to present. Starting at about $40,000 up to the present day $5.43 million. Certainly, an increase is understandable with the change in the economy, but fluctuations range from both the high end and the low end.

The conclusion of the entire paper states that politics are involved. The paper provides a brief history of the estate tax and its impact on the United States budget. It also examines ways in which the economic behavior of the affected population has changed over time in response to the market, technology, and political stimuli. Certainly, those variables, politics included, are involved. You need to plan for it because politics are always shifting.

Application of and Planning for the Estate Tax

Are the estate taxes administered when you make a will and trust, estate plan, and buy your investment vehicles? No, the estate tax is administered when someone passes. It's dependent on what the law was then, not what it is now or when drafting takes place and planning takes place. So how can you plan appropriately and correctly? A number of complicated strategies can help do that. To summarize, there are certain ways to pass assets outside of probate and shelter them from estate tax using instruments like trusts and trusts working in combination. There are ways to draft language into trusts that don't allow a lump sum to pass at one time and allow the recipient to receive income yearly, which is taxed as income tax. This avoids taking actual ownership of the entire lump sum property or the corpus of the trust, at one time. Do yourself a favor and consult both a financial planner and attorney regarding these matters and how they relate to you. I hope I've helped shed some light on why it might be important to plan for estate tax. Even though the estate tax limit might be high right now, that's just a brief snapshot in history.

Used Gift Exemption

When it comes to the federal laws surrounding estate tax exemption, there is a facet of the process known as the 'Used Gift Exemption'. If you have given any large gifts in your lifetime - i.e. monetary gifts that are large enough to be considered taxable - you will want to check how this impacts your exemption regarding estate tax payments. The larger the gift, the more you may have to pay in your estate tax bill because it takes away from the exemption you are allowed.

The taxable amounts are as follows: as a single person, if you have never gifted a party any amount of $14,000 (as of 2015), then you do not have to pay estate tax on it. As a married couple, this amount doubles; if you and your spouse have never gifted a figure of over $28,000, then again, you do not have to pay the estate tax on that amount. To give an example: if in 2015, as a single individual, say you give a family member a gift of $15,000, and then you pass away shortly after. The $1,000 is the amount that is subject to the taxation, since it exceeds the $14,000 amount (allowed for a single person) by $1,000. This is the used gift exemption amount. Note that any funds used to pay for someone's necessary expenses - for example, a school tuition or medical costs - are not included in these estate taxes as long as you paid the institutions directly.

That said, I do want to address charities, which many people I've encountered in my career graciously donate to, and then come to me with questions about the amounts that they have donated. Charitable contributions are not subject to the estate taxation; in fact, they help you decrease the amount you have to pay. If upon death you have given a certain amount of money to a charity, then the estate tax amount that's due is reduced by that very figure, dollar for dollar.[25]

Three Top Strategies and Best Practices

I wouldn't be known as the Elder Law Guy if I didn't offer some key strategies on how to plan and protect yourself, your family, and your prized assets from the estate taxes you might incur if you do not take the proper precautions. This chapter deals with the planning side, and so I want to give you some vehicles you can use to prepare. You might already do some of the things on this list, and if so, that's great; you are on your way to preparing and protecting your estate. But as I've learned through my career, you don't know what you don't know. So here are some best practices for safeguarding your hard earned property and assets:

1. Use a GRAT - a Grantor Retained Annuity Trust

A GRAT is one technique that estates have relied upon in the past to avoid paying or at least decrease the amount in tax liabilities when a parent passes estate assets to a son or daughter. The terms of the GRAT provide for the creation of an irrevocable trust between the person who is living and in possession of the estate and the beneficiary who will ultimately acquire the estate assets. First, the trust is created and the time period for the existence of the trust is established. Next, the estate assets are put under the terms of the trust, at which time the beneficiary begins to receive an annual annuity. Lastly, when the time period of the trust expires, the beneficiary is eligible to receive the assets, and this transaction happens completely free of tax.

A caveat of the GRAT, however, is that the time period for which the trust is established *must* not exceed the life of the individual who creates it - i.e. the elderly parent. If the parent creates the trust, and then passes away before the trust expires, then the son or daughter

[25]http://www.bankrate.com/calculators/tax-planning/estate-tax-planning-calculator.aspx

will not receive any of the assets, and those assets therefore are eligible to be taxed. This is why the process must be done as quickly as possible, and with a reasonable time frame in mind.[26]

2. Make a Charitable Contribution

You might already have charities to which you are contributing to regularly, and out of the goodness of your heart, you consider continuing the amount these organizations receive on your behalf even after you pass. The amount that you contribute to these charitable organizations can decrease the size of your estate, so it is therefore a win-win situation. This transfer of money from your estate to the charitable organization is known as a Lifetime Charitable Transfer, and is taken as a generous gift effective upon death.

Not only will the organization you hold near and dear to your heart be able to benefit from your very touching gift, your estate tax amount will also be reduced depending on the monetary amount you decide to leave to that group.

3. Consider a Family Limited Partnership

Throughout this book I have stressed the importance of relying upon family members and loved ones to help you in the planning process. Reduction of your estate taxes is another way where you can call upon these important people in your life, specifically with the implementation of a Family Limited Partnership. This allows the wealth you accumulated to be moved from your generation to the next. You would name those family members (who are the recipients of this wealth) to be the General Partners - those who participate in investment affairs - or Limited Partners - those who do not participate in the management or investment affairs.

Through the Family Limited Partnership (or FLP) the wealth and assets are held, and allow the participating members to contribute and pool resources. The assets pooled in the FLP are protected, and the senior family member can begin to transfer assets into the FLP to be used at a later date for children or grandchildren. Like the other two strategies, the FLP also reduces the amount that the estate is taxed.[27]

CHAPTER 9

Choose Wisely, Grasshopper: Selecting the Right Attorney and Firm

In the bustle of life, we set out with the best of intentions to work on our planning and preparation for what we may meet down the road. The many steps we must take to ensure our money, estate, assets, and families are secure can seem overwhelming, and can cause us to put off planning for those big life events that inevitably show up. This is a topic I want to address in detail.

I've been told if you create a visual to go with your goals, then everything you plan for is much more likely to happen. For instance, if you hang a vision board somewhere in your house, or pictures of what you want your future to look like - say a photo of a bigger house or an image of a nicer car - then psychologically, you are motivated to work that much harder for those things. As long as you're seeing those images each day, your goals will solidify in your mind. Many people have sworn by this technique, stating that it actually helped their plans and dreams to manifest.

The same can be said for Elder Law planning. If you know what you want to accomplish and what important facets of your life you want to protect down the line, then you can absolutely bring those dreams about with the right types of planning and organization.

However, the first question you have to ask yourself is: what exactly is your plan? Maybe you're still working every day, or perhaps you're in your 60s, 70s, or 80s, you've worked nearly your entire life, and now you want to enjoy your retirement.

Do you have enough money to make it through retirement? Maybe you do, but you want to make sure you can pass your legacy on to your children to make their lives easier, or pass on some farm land or your home.

Perhaps your children and grandchildren will be your main focus for what you do with your assets later in life. Do you want to help set up a college fund for your grandkids and make sure it's protected so the funds are only used to fund their higher education? How do you envision your hard-earned dollars helping them with whatever comes *their* way in life?

These are all possible when you plan ahead. The options then available to you should be taken into consideration as you begin this process. I always say, *nothing gets done unless it gets scheduled*. There's another saying that goes along with that, *if there's no intention, there's no tension*. That intention gets you there, whatever it is. So if you wanted to plan something, you should identify the steps needed to accomplish it, and write them on a calendar. Make sure they're scheduled so you devote your time to them.

When you carve out chunks of time from your day and make the effort to put them on a calendar, you are working to legitimize those steps and move your plan forward. Like a vision board, scheduling your tasks will make them more relevant and concrete in your mind. You wouldn't cancel a much-needed doctor's appointment or lunch with a close friend, would you? So why skip an appointment to plan for your future? There are other factors which will affect the efficiency of your planning, and we will review those in detail throughout this chapter.

Choose Wisely

It is crucial that the attorney and firm you choose take your planning and preparation goals as seriously as you do. Begin by taking a look at your assets and make sure you have your foundational documents in place. The ultimate goal is after all to save your hard-earned money and protect your assets, right?

Do you have the basics? Do you have the Power of Attorney? Do you possess a General Durable Power of Attorney, Healthcare Power of Attorney, Wills, Living Wills etc? What does your asset picture look like? Your attorney/firm might offer various planning tools, such as the one I offer my clients. It's an estate planning workbook, and I advise my clients to fill it out before our appointment. Ask your firm if they have a tool like this. I guarantee it will help keep you organized when it's time to talk about your assets during the appointment.

The One Constant in Life

I'd like to take this opportunity to ask a few questions and walk through a good thought process when you plan to save your hard earned money and property. Question one: What is the one constant in life? Well, the one constant in life is change. As much as we plan or think we know what will happen, we can guarantee that things will change. We can try to anticipate that change, but things are going to change regardless.

As I stated earlier, there is a two-thirds chance that if you're over 65, you may need some type of long term care in your life, whether at-home care, assisted living care, or nursing home care.

If your current health should change, you need to be prepared for how you'll pay for that. What are your options? What is your strategy to make sure you keep the money you've worked for? Maybe you're married. What's the strategy to make sure your assets for retirement, the income and property, aren't spent down, sold or liens placed on it because of a healthcare problem of you or your spouse? These are things we need to think about.

Think About Your Goals

Question two is, what are your goals? Are they to keep your land and money during your lifetime? Do you want to pass down your assets? Is there a farm you want to keep in the family? Is there a vacation property you want to make sure the family can still use after you're gone? What are your plans for that money and property?

I think we can all agree, change is constant and we need to plan. So, identify some goals for your healthcare options to protect your money and property to pass on, then to carry that further. This can be setting up trusts or something of that nature to help the grandkids go to college, or ensure your family is financially sound after your passing, and even so you're remembered when those major life events take place.

Goal Checklist:

Leave a Legacy for my Family?

_____

_____

Take Care of My Spouse When I'm Gone?

_____

_____

Save My Home?

_____

_____

Save My Other Properties?

_____

_____

Save My Investments?

_____

_____

Save My Retirement Savings?

_____

_____

Leave My Home and Money for Spouse?

_____

_____

Leave My Home and Money for Children?

_____

_____

Leave My Home and Money for Grandchildren?

_____

_____

Send Grandchildren to College?

_____

_____

Set Milestones to Distribute Monies to Grandchildren?

_____

_____

Leave Monies to My Church and/or Favorite Charity?

_____

_____

Reap the Rewards

What is your reward? What drives you? Is it knowing your grandkids, will go to college? Is it to have peace of mind, or sleep better, and have less stress because you know that binder on a shelf or in the safe holds all your important legal documents?

It might be your entire plan will grow with you. It might be you've already done everything under the law to take care of these things, and have peace of mind that things are taken care of. The property's protected, you have healthcare options. You have a plan in place. But are those enough? What about the attorney you choose?

Continuing Education

Not long before publication of this book, I attended an Elder Law immersion bootcamp in Tampa, Florida, to update myself on advanced planning and strategy techniques with attorneys from across the country. It was an incredible opportunity to speak with other professionals in my field and gain valuable new information for my clients.

One very important function of the boot camp was to bring us up to speed on changes to federal and state laws. This complicated area of law changes all the time, with constant updates to federal regulations and state Medicaid laws, tax laws, trust rules, and other things of that nature. So keeping up to date on those changes and learning cutting edge tools, strategies, new developments, new types of trusts, is a crucial component of the responsibilities of an Elder Law attorney, and you need to be aware of that when hiring an elder law attorney.

Networking

Another facet of the responsibility is communication. Communicating with leading attorneys nationwide who are passionate and know their stuff is a great way to bounce ideas and become inspired. Expanding my network outside of Shelby and the Charlotte area of North Carolina and seeing what other people from around the country are doing is a tremendous advantage, and is a tool all Elder Law attorneys should strive to utilize. It's so important to educate yourself in any profession, but it is definitely something to look at if you're searching for an attorney.

CHAPTER 10

The Role and Benefit of Technology in Elder Law

There is a huge benefit to incorporating technology into the care of senior citizens. When I work with seniors, there is an emotional component that hovers just below the surface, desperation. They know that something they have worked their entire lives to get is being threatened and may be taken from them. When we talk, my goal is to reassure them and explain in simple terms what we can do, and how to achieve this goal with clarity and ease. Technology can help do that.

As we talked about earlier, our main goals are to make sure our children and grandchildren are well taken care of financially, and can keep the home and the other parts of the estate when we pass. Money, however, is not the ultimate be-all-end-all goal, as I am sure you know. We all want to be remembered, and not only for the money and the assets we leave behind. We want to be remembered for the warmth and love in our hearts and the messages we leave through our legacy. They will know that even though we have passed on, we are still with them, alive and well in their hearts. What better way to leave them than with a keepsake that will last forever?

The days of seniors being computer and technology illiterate are long gone. I have found the senior of today regularly uses email to communicate, Facebook to keep up with the family, and online banking to pay bills, check balances and monitor retirement accounts and investments.

Using technology in an Elder Law practice to offer seniors the best possible service is not only a great option, it's becoming a necessity both to communicate with and provide top-notch, unique services to clients.

eDocs Access System Keeps your Important Documents at your Fingertips

Now that we've covered legacies, we will switch gears to feature another facet of technology invaluable to elder care: the eDocs Access System. This is a tool that has been extremely useful for McIntyre Elder Law. Essentially, it's an online bank-level security system allowing you to store important legal documents. The importance of keeping your documents safe, secure, and readily accessible can be a life-saving option, and we encourage all our clients to take advantage of the opportunity.

We will even upload our clients' documents for them to ensure the process is completed properly and quickly. Clients are thus able to share documents with any family member, whether they reside next door, out-of-state, or on the other side of the planet. The eDocs Access System doesn't send files as an e-mail attachment or across the open Internet and airways. It prompts all users to log-on, create a username and password, and then allows them to see only the documents the client makes available.

Your documents are therefore secure and held to international security standards. It's maintained with the same precautions as when you log into your online bank account.

The eDocs Access System has provided a tremendous benefit for clients that reside in other states. Clients can access the documents on an iPhone or other mobile device, such as the iPad or tablet. Clients are also provided with a laminated eDocs Access Card that can easily and securely be stored in any wallet. The card features the username, legal name, and even a spot where the password is listed. Of course, clients can opt to keep that space blank and simply remember the password so as not to risk losing the card and having the password out in the open.

I mentioned the importance of having documents on your person when I spoke about vacations. Imagine then this scenario: you have an emergency while traveling out of state, and you or a loved one has to go to the hospital. You have no documents on your person, yet you need to access some healthcare power of attorney documents, living will, or something like that.

With the eDocs Access System, all you do is pull out the card and go straight to the eDocs Access web link. Put in your username and password, and pull up those documents right there in the hospital or wherever you are. It works really, really well.

Steps to Leaving a Different Kind of Legacy

There are a couple of steps you can take to leave a different kind of legacy. I'm talking about a heart-filled memento your children and grandchildren will cherish for decades to come. At our office in Shelby, we invite our clients to record legacy videos. They can simply sit down and record one right in the comfort of our office. When they have completed the video, we put it onto a CD or load it on a USB drive that they can give to everybody in the family. They can even email it to their loved ones or put it on YouTube so there is a central location for people to view it. The options really are endless.

You need to do whatever you can to let your family know, this is what happened during your life. That's very important. By doing this, you give them more than just money or property.

What to Include in Legacy Videos

So what exactly do you put in a legacy video? It is really up to you, and of course, what you choose to include will depend on who the video is for. What do you want your children, grandchildren, and other family members to remember about you? What do you want them to get from watching the video? A legacy video can be your story brought to life. It can be anything from words of wisdom to tales about your childhood – anything you want your loved ones and family to remember you by.

The Priceless Benefits of Legacy Videos

Have you ever seen the movie *Brewster's Millions?* I always think of it when the topic of legacy videos come up. I'm specifically referencing the scene where they go to the attorney's wood panel office, and watch the great-uncle's video explaining how he'd like to dispose of his assets.

Now, that was a funny movie, but think about how powerful it is to have a traditional, old-fashioned will reading in that fashion. It could even be at your house, sitting around the den. You put on a DVD where mom, dad, grandma, or grandpa are talking to the family and saying, *"I love you guys. This is what I want you to do with my property, and my assets, and this is why I've done it this way".*

We live in a digital age, so that video could be on a USB drive or even stored in the 'Cloud'. It could be e-mailed to loved ones to view anytime and anywhere.

One of the best parts about your legacy isn't limited to just wills and assets. It's an opportunity to pass a little knowledge and heritage to the next generation. Just think how much wisdom you have to pass on after a lifetime lived.

If you lived through WWII, the Civil Rights Movement, JFK's assassination or the Apollo 11 moon landing, what was your experience of it? You can impart your memories and individual history to your children, your grandchildren, and beyond. Your morality, your wisdom, and how to act and why in situations can be elements to include, so your family can look back and understand the way things were for you. It's powerful in a lot of ways.

Our personal history is history. It's the story of us. How we got from then to now? How we went from a little colony of troublemakers to one of the most powerful nations on the planet? You can't grow if you don't know where you've come from, even if it's just a little thing – something seemingly insignificant.

There's a saying that you've probably heard by George Santayana which goes, *"Those who cannot remember the past are condemned to repeat it"*. We want to prevent that. We want to allow those experiences to pass forward and not be lost. That's what a legacy video could do.

The Simple Process of Creating a Legacy

So how exactly would we make a legacy video with one of our clients? Of course, the process will differ depending on the firm, but at my office we have steps to make it easy and straight forward. We have a team member meet with you either in your home or in the office. They set up the equipment and all you have to do is talk. Now sitting in front of a video camera can make people feel self-conscious, so it's always a good idea to prepare something in advance. You can read it over, get comfortable and feel confident before the recording takes place.

We like to set things up like an old fashioned tea party to feel at ease with each other. The expert will ask about you, and give you the chance to open up and tell your story to the camera. This is also their opportunity to learn about your experiences and how life has changed and progressed since your younger years, just as your family will learn later on.

Maybe you'll tell them about your career and the importance of hard work. Maybe you came from nothing, a real underdog, and overcame it to become a great success. This is your chance to tell that story to your children and grandchildren.

We'll show you the video first, so it can be edited any way you see fit. Maybe you don't want the kids to know everything – that's what editing is about. We just clip it out, it's that easy. Once you've got that video, it is something you can pass on to the entire family and generations to come.

The Importance of Constant Communication

During a trip to the Campbell Law School Library in Raleigh, North Carolina, I was inspired by the technology that I witnessed being used at the facility. Technology is no doubt a subject that people tend to shy away from, especially when pairing it with Elder Law. But technology does have a place in Elder Law. In my experience, the seniors I have as my clients are extremely up on technology: they're on Facebook; they navigate email; they do it all.

Transmission of information is key to keeping the lines of communication open with the seniors and other clients I welcome to my office. I make sure my website is chock full of user friendly features and important content that keeps my clients up to date on the ever-changing laws and legislation. We feature a variety of media such as video blogs and interviews to showcase experts in different fields of elder care. To ensure communication is consistent, I have established a newsletter sign-up right on the front page of the site. Clients and non-clients alike can enter their information and receive the latest news and information my company generates about Elder Law and the advances being made in that field.

It is key that seniors and other clients of any Elder Law firm remain in constant contact with the attorneys and the firm, so they stay informed and up-to-date on what's going on. Anything to facilitate communication is a huge benefit to seniors and their loved ones. The best Elder Law firms develop a culture which sparks excitement, interest, and facilitates communication.

Utilizing these tools, such as the eDocs Access System and legacy videos, acclimates you and your loved ones to the brilliant technology now available. They ensure your memories are kept safe and your loved ones secure with the assets, estate, and words of wisdom you provide for them for decades to come.

FREQUENTLY ASKED QUESTIONS

am always willing to answer any and all questions my clients pose to me regarding their Elder Law matters, legal proceedings, and any other general questions that might cross their minds during our conversations. For your benefit, I have compiled the top most frequently asked questions that I think really showcase the depth of knowledge that the clients crave.

Q: If I name my son or daughter as my primary power of attorney, will he/she be affected by my credit? And conversely, will his/her credit standing affect me in any way?

A: No, not at all. A power of attorney does not have any transfer effect or the ability to allow one person's credit to affect the other. While we are talking about powers of attorney, you do want to appoint somebody you totally trust as you attorney in fact. Another baseball reference that I talk about all the time is that you need to have people ready to come in off the bench, so you don't want to just have a primary there. If your primary power of attorney is unavailable, you want to have a secondary person come in and serve. Really if we do a document with primary, secondary, and maybe even a third person, then that document is going to live with you for a very long time and will hopefully be what you need that stays with you and works for you for the rest of your life. That's what we want it to do. So no matter the contingency or situation, it works.

Above all, your power of attorney needs to have a durability clause in it, so if you have a power of attorney right now, you need to read through it and make sure it says that it survives incapacity or incompetence. If it doesn't say that in the document, then it doesn't survive incapacity or incompetence. But the bottom line is, you will not be affected by your primary's credit, nor vice versa.

Q: Can't I just do all of this Elder Law planning by myself?

A: Well, you'd be gambling with everything that you've worked for your entire life. The law is unforgiving. The law doesn't care about your good intentions but only that the correct process was followed. You need a professional to do your important legal planning. You can't even afford to gamble on a semi-pro. So the question is, should you work an entire life, pay off a home and possibly other things, accumulate assets and then try to write your own will or plan for your retirement or try to save your estates on your own? And what would you use to keep track of everything, some type of software? To gamble it all on something that's $29.95 just doesn't make sense to me. You're going to get what you pay for. You need to make sure that you have the proper number of witnesses and a notary there to view the signing of the will. These witnesses have to see the testator sign the will in a line of sight manor. Witnesses should sign a self-proving affidavit avoiding these witnesses to be summoned by the court to testify that they witnessed the testator sign the will. Elder Law planning is not something you just breeze by. I tell people time and again: leave this to an expert. We're here to help you, trust me.

Q: When should I take my Social Security?

A: Take it as you head into your senior years, as it will help protect your assets and legacies. What I mean by this is you need to protect your home, your real estate, and the money that you saved for retirement. Protecting all of this also means that you need a financial adviser and planner who can answer the difficult questions for you.

The short answer is between the ages of 62 to 70. While you can take it anywhere along that timeline, there are advantages and disadvantages given your situation as to when you should take it.

According to my friend Jamie Richard, who is a financial advisor and wealth planner at Edward Jones Investment in Shelby, North Carolina, there are a few factors that determine the right time for you to take Social Security. They include:

▶ Life expectancy. This might be grim to think about, but consider your health. If you have very poor health, you probably want to go ahead and start taking it early on.

▶ Work status. Do you know when you plan to stop working? This will affect how much you can collect.

▶ Benefits. What will be the benefit if you wait until retirement age?

▶ Marital status. Single or married can have an effect on when you begin taking the Social Security, and how much you receive.

Remember that the longer you wait to take it, the greater your monthly checks will be. So if you start taking it at 62, you might get $1,000 a month. If you wait until 65, it might be $1,400 a month. If you want until you're 70, you may get $1,800 a month. Consider these factors with your financial advisor to determine when and if you should start taking Social Security.

Q: Can a parent's actions, documents and decisions be challenged?

A: Yes! Children can come in and challenge whether a senior is of sound mind when they drafted important legal documents. That is why planning ahead and solidifying important legal documents in place while one is still very sharp is very important.

Time is one of the enemies. I talk about titanic mistakes in elder law. That's one of the enemies: time. Waiting. People are motivated by fear, generally, and when they know that time crunch is on and they need to do something, it may be too late.

As a senior citizen, you do not want to find yourself in a hot potato situation, where nobody wants to take the responsibility. This means that when it comes time for your loved ones to speak on your behalf medically, you need to have identified the person the doctors and nurses are going to talk to. In a crisis situation, the less time you waste, the better. For this reason, it is crucial that you have those documents drafted and saved so that these important decisions cannot be challenged when you need them to be concrete.

Q: What if my will and/or other documents were drafted in another state?

A: Have an elder law attorney review these documents to make sure they have the fundamental elements for a will in North Carolina or your state. In North Carolina, for instance, you need to have two witnesses and a notary public see you sign the will by line of sight. That means they can't have looked away, can't be around the corner, and certainly can't be in the next room. If these three people do not see you sign the document, then it could be considered invalid in your respective state's court. In North Carolina, it would certainly be invalidated. To ensure that you are crossing all of your T's, speak with your trusted Elder Law attorney.

Q: After someone passes away, should I keep their paperwork?

A: Yes, save it. I try to save everything. It's a "just in case" measure in my opinion. Save it or scan it, save it digitally. I'm a huge fan of saving things digitally so we always have an exact copy to reproduce. If you prefer paper, then put it in a file drawer or keep it in a desk drawer. Digitally, you can throw it on a USB or a CD. But make sure you have it stored somewhere.

Q: If I don't have any debt, do I still have something to worry about?

A: Does not having a lot of debt protect against things like the Medicaid spend-down, paying large amounts of money for long-term care, or liens? I've had people with no debt and a couple of rental houses in their name ask me this question. They paid everything cash out-of-pocket and didn't have any mortgages, so what did they have to worry about?

My response to this question is simple: if you or your spouse have a long-term care event, and it costs you $75,000 to $100,000 per year to pay for that care indefinitely, is that going to put a dent in your finances? Are the rental houses still going to be okay? Is the bank account still going to be okay? Are the monies that you have in savings going to be okay?

The answer is no. It doesn't matter how much money you have. At that rate of a spend-down, you're not going to be okay. It's going to be very hard for you to maintain your lifestyle and your savings if you're spending down money at that rate.

What should you do to get some protection? Well, just from my experience and knowledge of Elder Law, my initial recommendation is that you need to separate that liability with the rental houses and the personal income.

Are you or your husband veterans? Did you serve one day during war time? You may easily qualify for Veterans Aid and Attendance benefits, which could add up to $2,500 to $2,750 per month to your income. That could help out a lot if you had some type of long-term care situation.

Do you have your foundations in place? Do you have your general durable power of attorney, healthcare power of attorney, living will, and will? Is there anything to talk about there? It was great that you were shrewd with your money, but have you been shrewd and prudent with your legal planning and protective legal planning strategies?

Consider these questions, as I suggest to my clients. Layer up on your protection of your assets, because at the end of the day, you are still going to have to make some tough decisions should you fall into a healthcare crisis, debt or no debt.

Q:What If My Attorney-In-Fact Predeceases Me?

A: I look at this situation like a ball game. If the first attorney-in-fact you appointed fouls out, you need to have somebody coming off the bench to take that person's place. If that next person fouls out, is unable or unwilling to serve, then you need to have another person coming in off the bench to take that second person's place.

In my opinion, you should go two to three people deep for subs. You have to have a deep bench, so that document grows with you and lasts throughout your entire life.

Just in case, heaven forbid, your husband or wife passed away and was unable to serve as your attorney-in-fact, for your business or personal affairs or healthcare decisions, you automatically have that trusted son or daughter coming in to handle those affairs for you.

You don't need to have that document redone or have any new legal work done if that husband or wife, that first person that you had in there, passes away. The document should be written as such. Should my wife be unwilling or unable to serve – and name your wife – then I nominate or designate my daughter – her name – to serve as my lawful attorney-in-fact in her stead.

We could add other people in there, so that we have people to take the primary attorney-in-fact's place.

Q: What if I already have a will?

A: This one may be the most common questions I get. It's not so much a question as a statement or belief. Some of my clients already had their wills done, so they think they're protected.

Having your will in place is great. But I know that there's a 7 out of 10 chance that everybody over 65 right now is going to need some type of long-term care throughout their life – whether it be in-home, assisted living, or nursing home care – based on our healthcare technology and the age of people right now in the population. That's just the facts according to a 2005 US Department of Health and Human Services report.

So if you have a will, that is great. I'd love to take a look at that will and make sure it's up to snuff. I do that all the time, just to check those documents out. But if we're passing your home, for instance, through your will, then we open it up to a probate estate down at the courthouse. You have to go down to the courthouse. You have to pay to open the estate. You have to publish it in the paper, most times, and then wait 90 days. That's not for people to throw money into your estate, so you have more there, but for people to attach liens, like Medicaid liens or liens for healthcare costs the last year of your life.

Any lien, any debt that has been unpaid, comes in on the estate. Your property could be sold to pay for that lien. We see it happen all the time. So I'm glad you have a will, but to me, the will is just the safety net. It's there to catch whatever we don't directly make transferable upon death assets, which travel outside of the probate estate directly to your beneficiary.

Again, layer up on the protection and you won't find yourself with your hands tied when you actually need them to be free.

GLOSSARY OF TERMS

Legal Tools

Caregiver Contract

The agreement, also known as personal service or personal care agreements, is essentially an employment contract between the caregiver and the recipient of care. A caregiver agreement stipulates a caregiver's tasks, the hours spent caregiving and financial compensation for the family caregiver. (1)

Deed

A written instrument, which has been signed and delivered, by which one individual, the grantor, conveys title to real property to another individual, the grantee; a conveyance of land, tenements, or hereditaments, from one individual to another. (2)

Durable Power of Attorney

A special type of power of attorney that is used frequently is the "durable" power of attorney. A durable power of attorney differs from a traditional power of attorney in that it continues the agency relationship beyond the incapacity of the principal. The two types of durable power of attorney are immediate and "springing." The first type takes effect as soon as the durable power of attorney is executed. The second is intended to "spring" into effect when a specific event occurs, such as the disability of the principal. Durable powers of attorney have become popular because they enable the principal to have her or his affairs handled easily and inexpensively after she or he has become incapacitated. (3)

Enhanced Life Estate Deed/Ladybird Deed

This deed is similar to a traditional life estate deed in that the grantor retains access to the property during life. However, the enhanced life estate deed includes the grantor's right to use the property in any legal way, including the option to change the final beneficiary (grantee) without any additional consent from the original remainderman. The grantor also retains the ability to sell or mortgage the property and keep all of the proceeds without any penalty for waste. (4)

General Warranty Deed

An instrument transferring ownership of real property, and which warrants—promises—that the seller has good title with no adverse claimants and that the seller will defend the title against other parties should that prove necessary. (5)

Health Care Power of Attorney

The legal transfer of the authority to make medical decisions on behalf of another person. That is, health care power of attorney gives the designee (called an agent) the ability to determine what medical procedures may be done on the principal in the event of the principal's incapacitation. (6)

Intentionally Defective Grantor Trust

This trust treats the assets in the trust differently for income tax purposes than for estate tax and gift tax purposes. The veteran will be the grantor but not a beneficiary. This trust will take advantage of the Internal Revenue Code Sections 671-677, and takes advantage of the differential tax treatment for income tax purposes. For most veterans, the major asset in this trust is the residence. If the veteran owns the residence as an individual and sells it, then the proceeds will be part of the veterans Net Worth and will disqualify the veteran for the VA Pension Benefit. However, if the residence is in the trust and sold by the trustee of the trust, the proceeds from the sale of the house is not imputed to the veteran by VA. (7)

Irrevocable Life Insurance Trust

Death benefits from life insurance policies are not subject to income tax. But the benefits could be counted as part of your taxable estate, and if life insurance proceeds push your estate value above the exemption level, the government will hand your beneficiaries a potentially large tax bill. An irrevocable life insurance trust is a tool that can help beneficiaries erase the tax burden. The trust "owns" your life insurance policy, pays the premiums and gives the death benefit to your beneficiaries when you die. By placing ownership of the policy with a trust — not the insured — it removes the death benefit from your estate. (8)

Irrevocable Living Trust

A trust into which a grantor deposits assets for use by a beneficiary where the terms of the trust cannot be modified or abrogated without permission of the beneficiary. That is, when a grantor sets up an irrevocable trust, he/she completely relinquishes ownership of the assets placed in the trust. As a result, an irrevocable trust is not usually considered part of the grantor's estate for estate tax purposes. (9)

Life Estate Deed

A life estate is where a natural person owns all the benefits of ownership in the property during their life, or the life of another, with the property going to a remainder person after the death of the life tenant. It is an interest in real or personal property that is limited in duration to the lifetime of its owner or some other designated person or persons. (10)

Limited Power of Attorney

The authority granted to another under a written power of

attorney, specifying or describing the particular acts the attorney in fact may do, and no others. Contrast with a general power of attorney, which allows all things the person could do himself or herself. Limited powers are usually given to do things like transfer stock, obtain information from the IRS or Social Security Administration, sign all documents necessary for a real estate closing, or other such tasks. (11)

Living trust

A trust created for the trustor and administered by another party during the trustor's lifetime. The living trust may be formed because the trustor is either incapable of managing or unwilling to manage his or her assets. The trust can be revocable or irrevocable, depending upon the trustor's wishes. Also called inter vivos trust. (12)

Living will

A document specifying the kind of medical care a person wants- or does not want-in the event of terminal illness or incapacity. (13)

Long-Term Care

Long-term medical care for a debilitating but non-life threatening condition. For example, one may require long-term care if one is involved in a car accident or has a non-terminal disease that does not allow him/her to live independently. Long-term care often involves the inability to perform at least some of the activities of daily living. (14)

Medicaid Asset Protection Trust

A valuable tool that many people implement with their estate planning to protect their assets while still qualifying for Medicaid. This trust allows you to transfer assets to a special kind of trust where you are not the trustee and not the principal beneficiary, but still have access to income from the trust, thereby allowing you to qualify after a look back period. (15)

Medicaid Compliant Annuity

The Medicaid Compliant Annuity was designed to convert a spend-down amount into an income stream. With the spend-down amount eliminated, the nursing home resident/Medicaid applicant becomes eligible for Medicaid benefits. Essentially, a Medicaid Compliant Annuity is a period certain single immediate annuity with an added restrictions endorsement. (16)

Power of Attorney

A written document in which one person (the principal) appoints another person to act as an agent on his or her behalf, thus conferring authority on the agent to perform certain acts or functions on behalf of the principal. Powers of attorney are routinely granted to allow the agent to take care of a variety of transactions for the principal, such as executing a stock power, handling a tax audit, or maintaining a safe-deposit box. Powers of attorney can be written to be either general (full) or limited to special circumstances. A power of attorney generally is terminated when the principal dies or becomes incompetent, but the principal can revoke the power of attorney at any time. (17)

Promissory Note

A written promise made by one party to make a stated payment in full by a certain date. A promissory note is a binding, legal contract. (18)

Quitclaim Deed

A deed releasing the interest or ownership, if any, that the writer, known as a grantor, has in a property. It is important to note that a quitclaim deed does not attest that the grantor actually has an ownership interest in the property; it merely states that the grantor no longer claims to have one. One who buys a property in exchange for a quitclaim deed therefore accepts the possibility that another person or persons have an ownership interest in it. For this reason, some property insurance companies do not providecoverage for a property with only a quitclaim deed. (19)

Revocable Living Trust

A revocable living trust is a popular estate planning tool that you can use to determine who will get your property when you die. Most living trusts are "revocable" because you can change them as your circumstances or wishes change. Revocable living trusts are "living" because you make them during your lifetime. (20)

Special Warranty Deed

A special warranty deed is a deed in which the seller warrants or guarantees the title only against defects arising during the period of his or her tenure or ownership of the property. The grantor makes no warranty against defects existing before the time of his or her ownership. (21)

Supplemental Needs Trust

This is a US-specific term for a type of special needs trust (an internationally recognized term). Supplemental needs trusts are compliant with provisions of US state and federal law and are designed to provide benefits to, and protect the assets of, physically disabled or mentally disabled persons and still allow such persons to be qualified for and receive governmental health care benefits, especially long-term nursing care benefits, under the Medicaid welfare program. Supplemental or Special Needs Trusts are frequently used to receive an inheritance or personal injury litigation proceeds on behalf of a disabled person in order to allow the person to qualify for Medicaid benefits. (22)

Tenants in Common

Two or more persons who own property together with no rights of survivorship. That is, when one of the co-owners dies, his/her share of the property becomes part of his/her estate and passes on to heirs. Tenants in common may own equal or unequal shares of the property. (23)

Testamentary Trust

A trust created in a will. A testamentary trust is considered part of an estate and is therefore subject to estate taxes, if any. However, a testamentary trust is useful if the deceased has minor children whose assets need to be managed before they reach maturity. The trustee of the testamentary trust does this on behalf of the estate. (24)

Trust

A legal arrangement whereby control over property is transferred to a person or organization (the trustee) for the benefit of someone else (the beneficiary). Trusts are created for a variety of reasons, including tax savings and improved asset management. (25)

Warranty Deed

A deed is a written instrument that transfers the title of property from one person to another. Although many types of deeds exist, title is usually transferred by a warranty deed. A warranty deed provides the greatest protection to the purchaser because the grantor (seller) pledges or warrants that she legally owns the property and that there are no outstanding liens, mortgages, or other encumbrances against it. A warranty deed is also a guarantee of title, which means that the seller may be held liable for damages if the grantee (buyer) discovers the title is defective. There are two types of warranty deeds: general and special. (26)

Will

A will is the legal instrument that permits a person, the testator, to make decisions on how his estate will be managed and distributed after his death. (27)

Financial Assets

401 K

You participate in a 401(k) retirement savings plan by deferring part of your salary into an account set up in your name. Any earnings in the account are federal income tax deferred. There are two types of 401 (k), traditional and Roth. With a traditional 401(k), you defer pretax income, which reduces the income tax you owe in the year you made the contribution. You pay tax on all withdrawals at your regular rate. With the newer Roth 401(k), which is offered in some but not all plans, you contribute after-tax income. Earnings accumulate tax deferred, but your withdrawals are completely tax free if your account has been open at least five years and you're at least 59 1/2. In either type of 401(k), you can defer up to the federal cap, plus an annual catch-up contribution if you're 50 or older. With a 401(k), you are responsible for making your own investment decisions by choosing from among investment alternatives offered by the plan. Those alternatives typically include separate accounts, mutual funds, annuities, fixed-income investments, and sometimes company stock (28)

529 Accounts

An account into which persons deposit funds to save for university-related expenses. The funds in a 529 college savings account are tax-deferred and, if used directly to pay for college, tax exempt at the federal level. They are sometimes exempt at the state level as well. The plan exists in an attempt to make post-secondary education more affordable. (29)

Annuity

A regular, periodic payment made by an insurance company to a policy holder for a specified period of time. (30)

Bonds

Bonds are debt securities issued by corporations and governments. Bonds are, in fact, loans that you and other investors make to the issuers in return for the promise of being paid interest, usually but not always at a fixed rate, over the loan term. The issuer also promises to repay the loan principal at maturity, on time and in full. Because most bonds pay interest on a regular basis, they are also described as fixed-income investments. While the term bond is used generically to describe all debt securities, bonds are specifically long-term investments, with maturities longer than ten years. (31)

Certificate of Deposits

CDs are time deposits. When you purchase a CD from a bank, up to $100,000 is insured by the Federal Deposit Insurance Corporation (FDIC). You generally earn compound interest at a fixed rate, which is determined by the current interest rate and the CD's term, which can range from a week to five years. (32)

Custodial Accounts

An account at a bank, brokerage, or insurance company held by an adult guardian on behalf of a minor child. That is, the minor child owns the custodial account, but the parent or guardian manages it and makes all decisions related to it. The child takes control of the account at a certain age: 18, 21, or 25, depending on the jurisdiction. Importantly, the account is taxed at the guardian's marginal tax rate until the child turns 18, at which point it is taxed at the child's rate. (33)

Money Market

The segment of the financial markets in which highly liquid short term assets trade; the money market is used by participants as a means to borrow and lend on a short-term basis from several days to just under a year. Money market securities consist of negotiable certificates of deposit (CDs), bankers acceptances, U.S. Treasury bills, commercial paper, municipal notes, federal funds, and repurchase agreements (repos). (34)

Mutual Funds

An investment instrument that is made up of a pool of funds collected from many investors for the purpose of investing in securities such as stocks, bonds, money market instruments, and similar assets. Mutual funds are operated by money managers, who actively manage a fund's assets in an attempt to produce positive returns for the fund's investors. A mutual fund's portfolio strategy is structured and maintained to match the investment objectives stated in its prospectus. (35)

Roth IRA

An investment retirement account in which a worker makes non-tax deductible contributions up to a certain limit throughout his/her working life. Unlike traditional IRAs, withdrawals are tax-free but contributions are not deductible. The limit to annual contributions varies by year according to inflation ($5,000 in 2008 and 2009). Roth IRAs are allowed to invest in securities and, in practice, normally own common stock and certificates of deposit. (36)

Securities

A document; historically, a physical certificate but increasingly electronic, showing that one owns a portion of a publicly-traded company or is owed a portion of a debt issue. Securities are tradable. At their most basic, securities refer to stocks and bonds, but the term sometimes also refers to derivatives such as futures and options. (37)

Stocks

A security that represents ownership in a corporation and has claims on part of the corporation's assets and earnings per share.

There are two main types of stock: (1) common and (2) preferred. (1) Common stock usually entitles the owner to vote at shareholders' meetings and receive dividends when applicable. (2) Preferred stock generally does not include voting rights but has a priority claim on assets and earnings ahead of common shares. (38)

Traditional IRA

A tax-deferred individual retirement account that allows annual contributions of up to $2000 for each income earner. Contributions are fully deductible for all individuals who are not active participants in employer-sponsored plans or for plan participants within certain income ranges. (39)

Trust Account

A bank account specially designated to hold funds that belong to others. Real estate brokers and attorneys are required to maintain separate trust accounts for client money and for escrowed funds. (40)

Unit Trust

An unincorporated mutual fund structure that allows funds to hold assets and pass profits through to the individual owners, rather than reinvesting them back into the fund. The investment fund is set up under a trust deed. The investor is effectively the beneficiary under the trust. (41)

US Saving Bonds

In the United States, a non-tradable bond issued by the federal government for savings purposes. A savings bond allows citizens to receive a guaranteed return for their investments and helps raise revenue for the government. (42)

CHECKLISTS:

Checklist for Veterans Aid & Attendance Benefits:

Veteran? Spouse of Veteran? Spouse of deceased veteran?

_____

_____

_____

At least 90 days of active duty service?

_____

_____

At least one day of active duty service during a wartime event. Service does not have to be in a combat theater?

_____

_____

_____

Under $20,000 in assets, excluding home. Consult an Elder Law Attorney for strategic legal planning and advice?

_____

_____

_____

A current need: At least 2 out of 6 standard ADLs impaired? ADLs:

- ▶ **Eating?**
- ▶ **Preparing Meals?**
- ▶ **Walking?**
- ▶ **Dressing?**
- ▶ **Bathing?**
- ▶ **Toileting?**

A physician must sign an FL2 form confirming current need.

_____

_____

_____

Goal Checklist:

Leave a Legacy for my Family?

Take Care of My Spouse When I'm Gone?

Save My Home?

Save My Other Properties?

Save My Investments?

Save My Retirement Savings?

Leave My Home and Money for Spouse?

Leave My Home and Money for Children?

Leave My Home and Money for Grandchildren?

Send Grandchildren to College?

Set Milestones to Distribute Monies to Grandchildren?

Leave Monies to My Church and/or Favorite Charity?

END NOTES FOR GLOSSARY OF TERMS

1. http://www.bankrate.com/finance/personal-finance/reasons-to-sign-caregiver-agreement.aspx

2. http://legal-dictionary.thefreedictionary.com/deeds

3. http://legal-dictionary.thefreedictionary.com/Durable+power+of+attorney

4. https://www.deeds.com/information/Enhanced-Life-Estate-Ladybird-Deed-vs-Traditional-Life-Estate-Deed-1349119046.html

5. http://financial-dictionary.thefreedictionary.com/General+Warranty+Deed

6. http://financial-dictionary.thefreedictionary.com/Healthcare+Power+of+Attorney

7. http://www.experts123.com/q/what-is-va-pension-benefit-asset-protection-trust.html

8. http://www.insure.com/life-insurance/trusts.html

9. http://financial-dictionary.thefreedictionary.com/Irrevocable+trust

10. http://definitions.uslegal.com/r/real-estate-reservation-life-estate-deeds/

11. http://financial-dictionary.thefreedictionary.com/Limited+power+of+attorney

12. http://financial-dictionary.thefreedictionary.com/living+trust

13. http://financial-dictionary.thefreedictionary.com/living+will

14. http://financial-dictionary.thefreedictionary.com/
   Long+term+care

15. http://www.sinclairprosserlaw.com/trustee-medicaid-asset-
   protection-trust/

16. http://www.meritins.com/pdfs/MedicaidSPIA.pdf

17. http://financial-dictionary.thefreedictionary.com/
   power+of+attorney

18. http://financial-dictionary.thefreedictionary.com/
   Promissary+note

19. http://financial-dictionary.thefreedictionary.com/
   quitclaim+deed

20. http://www.nolo.com/legal-encyclopedia/revocable-living-
   trusts.html

21. http://www.investopedia.com/terms/s/special-warranty-deed.
   asp

22. http://encyclopedia.thefreedictionary.com/
   Supplemental+Needs+Trust

23. http://financial-dictionary.thefreedictionary.com/
   Tenants+in+Common

24. http://financial-dictionary.thefreedictionary.com/
   Testamentary+Trust

25. http://financial-dictionary.thefreedictionary.com/trust

26. http://legal-dictionary.thefreedictionary.com/warranty+deed

27. http://legal-dictionary.thefreedictionary.com/Will

28. http://financial-dictionary.thefreedictionary.com/401k

29. http://financial-dictionary.thefreedictionary.
   com/529+College+Savings+Plan

30. http://financial-dictionary.thefreedictionary.com/annuities

31. http://financial-dictionary.thefreedictionary.com/bonds

32. http://financial-dictionary.thefreedictionary.com/CD

33. http://financial-dictionary.thefreedictionary.com/
custodial+account

34. http://financial-dictionary.thefreedictionary.com/
Money+Market

35. http://financial-dictionary.thefreedictionary.com/mutual+funds

36. http://financial-dictionary.thefreedictionary.com/Roth+IRA

37. http://financial-dictionary.thefreedictionary.com/securities

38. http://financial-dictionary.thefreedictionary.com/Stocks

39. http://financial-dictionary.thefreedictionary.com/
traditional+IRA

40. http://financial-dictionary.thefreedictionary.com/trust+account

41. http://www.investopedia.com/terms/u/unittrust.asp

42. http://financial-dictionary.thefreedictionary.com/
United+States+savings+bond

ABOUT THE AUTHOR

Greg McIntyre lives in Shelby, North Carolina (outside of Charlotte, NC) with his wife of 17 years and their 6 children. Greg initially became a lawyer to fight courtroom battles which he did for years. However, after working in an environment where the focus was always on the next billable hour, he started his own practice because he was interested in being more than just a lawyer. Greg was interested in making a difference in his client's lives.

Being a husband and a father taught Greg what was really important in life. Greg takes pride in building trust with his clients and feels they share the same values. Greg strives to help others leave a legacy to be preserved and to have a guiding hand in shaping their families' lives.

Memberships and Associations.

Greg is a veteran of the United State's Navy and a member of the North Carolina State Bar Association. He is a member of ElderCounsel, a national network focused specifically on estate planning & wealth preservation. He serves on the Board of Directors of the Boys & Girls Club, Cleveland County Counsel on Aging, Journey and ACCES. He is a proud member of and Deacon at Shelby Presbyterian Church, where he and his family find fellowship and spiritual refreshment.

Made in the USA
Monee, IL
11 May 2021